INSIDE RECOVERY

INSIDE RECOVERY

Our DREAMS and the TWELVE STEPS

Wayne M.

With acknowledgement and heartfelt gratitude for the Twelve Steps of Alcoholics Anonymous, which have made recovery from addiction available to millions.

Publisher:
Growing Edge Books

Editor:
Kevin Hanlon

Cover Design:
Danny Loi

Cover Photo:
Iakov Filimonov/Dreamstime

ISBN: 978-0-578-31023-7

insideourrecovery.com

Dedication:

To Kevin Hanlon, my editor and friend,
without whose encouragement and support
this book would never have happened.

CONTENTS

WE ADDICTS

We addicts never really thought there would be consequences. Somehow, magically, our addictions would take care of any fears and uncomfortable feelings we might have. Things would always turn out just fine.

We could drink until our insides ruptured. We could control and manipulate until we lost our humanity. We could eat or restrict until our organs shut down. We could gamble until we were beyond ruin. We could rage and hate until we choked on our own bile, have sex until we had numbed all disgust, smoke crack until we were less than nothing, use opioids until we were a void, work until we could value nothing, and do coke until we were no longer mortal.

We were invincible—until we were not. And the reckoning was agonizing beyond anything we could imagine.

While we were putting ourselves through all of this, somewhere inside us there was a tenacious spark of awareness left, a piece of ourselves that just might possibly be enough to save us. What shred of consciousness was still there?

We lost all our connection with an inner life, but something human inside us still dreamed.

TO YOU, THE READER

I would like to talk to you about your dreams. Not your aspirations and fantasies, but literally the dreams you had last night and have already forgotten. The dreams you have had every night of your life. They often seem to mock us, teasing our waking consciousness and, before we know it, slipping away into nothingness. What are we to make of them? Why are we so eager to ignore them?

I want to talk with you about what I have learned about the value of dreams as a tool of recovery, so I would like our conversation to be from one recovering addict to another. We know all too well what it means to juggle states of mind, the overwhelming struggle between the day-to-day world we cannot change and the elusive reality of what is going on inside us. That conundrum is what nearly destroyed each of us. But we learn it doesn't need to. It is actually what gives life its spark and resonance.

Our Twelve Step Programs are written in the past tense, a record of what works. They are meant to offer us guidance on how to live in the world, while staying true to our visceral inner responses and our system of values at the same time, without having to turn to the deadening comfort promised by our addictions. How do we manage to act as the people we always knew we were meant to be before all the drama and destruction?

It is hard work and I, for one, need a lot of help. Also, I get confused very easily. What is the guidance I can really trust? I talk to my sponsor. I pay attention at meetings. I pray and meditate to the best of my ability on any given day. But I always end up wondering if what I come up with is really the last word. What have I missed? I always get the sense that I have somehow failed to access the clear and definitive message from within that I crave and that I need. I seem to be the kind of person who needs something tangible to meditate "on." But what?

Dreams were never my first answer. Only gradually did I realize that they might be exactly the inexhaustible, living object of contemplation that I was searching for. So much elaborate misinformation has been spun around them since the end of the 19th Century. Our dreams have largely been stolen from us as basic human tools of guidance and enlightenment that we can use when we want to. Instead they have become the province of well-meaning white, male theorists, self-proclaimed "experts," claiming to be the only ones able to interpret our dreams for us using their various proprietary systems of thought, at great expense to us and our insurance companies. The goal of much of their writing on dreams was to get themselves taken seriously by the scientific and medical communities, and by the public. It worked to the exclusion of almost all other approaches.

Freud was the first to describe the interpretation of dreams as "the royal road to a knowledge of the unconscious activities of the mind,"[1] presumably open and unobstructed, a broad direct path inwards. But then, in his excitement, he declared that only he and his disciples could explain them according to an idiosyncratic and highly sexualized framework he constructed. Any failure to understand a

---

[1] Sigmund Freud, *The Interpretation of Dreams* (New York: Avon Books, 1965), 647.

dream was put down to a form of Victorian repression in the dreamer. It was assumed at the time that the dreamers (mostly women at first) were too limited, too frightened to deal with the images that they themselves had created.

Contrast that with those of us who are addicts in recovery and have had the courage to take moral ownership of everything in us, everything we got right, and everything we got wrong. (Step Four.) We are ready for anything our dreams might throw at us. Just bring them on.

Jung, one of Freud's most successful competitors, made a valiant effort to subjugate all aspects of dreams to his intellect and to his passion for order. He was fascinated by the ways the imagery of various civilizations and, indeed, the whole history of human thought and imagination showed up in dreams. Well, of course they do, but they don't necessarily need to be applied to every dream. Jung also entertained the intriguing, but unproven, hypothesis that there might be a consciousness that links all minds and that there is a set of universal, "archetypical" symbols common to all mankind. Perhaps. But no matter how appealing his grand concepts might be, they might just as well be explained as a reflection of the dazzlingly complex structure of the brain itself. Too much brilliant speculation runs the risk of separating us from the content of our actual dreams. Even Jung said that when he started to work with a dream he needed to set his theories aside and listen to the dream itself.[2] That makes sense. We can do the same thing. As addicts we have learned that we recover in specifics, and that we need to deal with each situation that arises in our lives on its own terms. It turns out we too need to calm our busy minds and deal with specific

---

[2] C.G. Jung, *Memories, Dreams, Reflections* (New York: Vintage Books, 1989), 170.

details of our dreams exactly as they present themselves as well.

These two giants in the study and interpretation of dreams and others like them made huge strides in getting the world at large to pay attention to the inner life, but they left little room for those who came after them and have taken a more modest approach to dreams as a discussion between equals. For the most part the only people talking about their dreams today outside of therapists' offices are individuals or small anonymous groups who carry on the tradition, as old as humankind, of recounting them randomly to anyone who will listen. This happens from time to time at Twelve Step meetings and in our recovery work when someone blurts out that they just had a dream and don't know what to do with it. We instinctively know it must be significant, but the best response we can come up with is a puzzled silence. What are we missing?

It is worth remembering that before we were inundated with the relentless torrent of media images that swamp us now, the most vivid and arresting event in any day was probably the dream each of us woke up with. Put in contemporary terms, our dreams have always been understood as "selfies" of our inner life. Do we really want to ignore them, we who, in recovery, are going to such pains to find inner guidance that will help us deal with our damaged relationship to the outer world? How we can take back our dreams?

We know from experience the danger of "contempt prior to investigation." What if our dreams are a form of communication? What if the estimated 86 billion neurons, a similar number of glia and over a trillion synapses in our brains are processing more than our conscious minds can fathom, revealing awarenesses to us in sleep that are available nowhere else? [3] Instead of asserting, as Freud did, that there is a huge, murky and menacing unconscious mind within us, what if we were to consider that there is a dynamic, creative mind at work in us, trying to reveal itself? That would be consistent with our understanding of the kind of world that is presented in the Twelve Steps, one in which we are cared for and provided with inner guidance. We have a choice of which view fits best with our own experience and understanding.

Whenever I doubt my conviction that dreams are communications, I need to remind myself that every time I sit down to discuss a current dream with someone, one-on-one or in a group of people I have never met, within ten minutes we find ourselves talking about the most pressing and important issues of our lives. This is no coincidence. We have allowed the dream to speak.

Not to say that the messages are initially obvious, although they become more so with time. Usually they are elusive, and no wonder, given how long we have ignored them and treated them with disrespect. No wonder they do not reveal their messages bluntly without proper attention being paid. This is not Freudian repression, but the mind protecting itself from the ruthless need of our consciousness to dominate everything within us and reduce it all to something we can conquer and explain.

There is almost always at least one element of a dream that makes no sense at all and yet breathes life into it. This seemingly random surprise reminds us that we are in another realm with a logic of its own, one that we will never quite understand. Our dreams are dynamic. They want us to pay

---

[3] Ferris Jabr, "To Unlock the Brain's Mysteries, Purée It," *New York Times*, Dec. 21, 2017.

attention to them and we can actually watch them become more energetic as we begin to treat them with interest and respect.

One particularly challenging type of dream for those of us who are addicts is the "lucid dream," where we dream we are conscious while we are in the dream itself and believe we can change its outcome through the force of our own cleverness and willpower. It can be quite a heady experience. Such dreams are a glimpse into truly mind-boggling levels of consciousness and that makes them particularly attractive to us as addicts who have spent a lifetime trying to prove how special we are.

Inevitably we will be tempted to focus on the extraordinary and dismiss all our other dreams as too pedestrian to be bothered with. This is a mistake. We can only deal with the pyrotechnics of the mind when we have first gotten comfortable with the idea that our dreams are an important part of coming to terms with the life that is right in front of us.

Of course when we look at a dream months or years after having written it down, the protections have mostly fallen away and we cannot believe that we could have missed how obvious it was. Like the oracles in stories from antiquity, the confusion they create only lasts long enough for a hidden truth to emerge.

The challenge with treating dreams as communications is that, to our conscious minds, they are "weird." (Everybody has the same reaction.) They seem to speak in another language, one without the neat, agreed-upon grammatical arrangement of words that we use in our everyday life. So what is their language, and how can we learn it?

Fortunately, those of us in recovery are having the experience of learning a new working language to understand our lives. The Steps reveal things in us that we don't want to know but have to come to terms with if we want to survive. Dreams do the same and they have their own set of rather basic techniques, principles and even slogans for understanding them. These will emerge as we look at a series of dreams in the following chapters and see how they can shed light from within on the way our lives are unfolding.

One of the biggest obstacles to working with our dreams is the common refrain, proudly announced, especially among men, "I never dream." That is not possible. We all do. Just try not sleeping and dreaming for a few days. We go nuts. Our dreams turn out to be part of a little-understood ecosystem of balance and sanity within us and we can't do without them.

What we can learn is how to capture them. The first technique is not to move until we have firmly fixed at least one image from the dream in our minds when we wake up. While we are dreaming the body turns off its motor functions or we would be thrashing around acting out what we are experiencing. If we move a muscle we are literally shaking the dream loose.

As soon as we have one image solidly in mind, it is time to move just enough to write it down immediately. Other images usually follow, sometimes layered on each other, until the whole dream comes back to us. This can be frustrating at first, but with practice it can become almost second nature. Our dreams seem to appreciate the attention and respond to it by being more communicative and more available. (There will still be periods, as there are for all of us, when mysteriously we can't remember any of our dreams no matter what we do. These will pass.)

Our dreams also can feel like a threat to us in other ways. They challenge our impoverished but deeply-held addict's

view of what it is to be a human being. They make us
uncomfortable and we want to dismiss them. It is
inconceivable to us that in the vast experiment of homo-
sapiens and mammals on earth we should have evolved an
inner maker of dreams. We addicts are determined to be one-
dimensional at all costs, but our dreams won't tolerate our
desire to be less than we are.

They are a reminder of how much we do not know and
cannot control. We don't even know where intuitions come
from, or fully-formed ideas that pop into our waking minds
as if from outside us. All these clues to how wondrous and
complex we are definitely are not welcome. And this is long
before we are challenged to come to terms with the much
bigger issue of a power greater than ourselves in the Twelve
Steps.

Our dreams will allow us to ignore the beauty and
mystery of our inner life for only so long. Their messages of
health are insistent and always as close to us as our pillow.
They are always at the ready, especially when we take on
something as monumental and life-altering as recovery from
our addictions.

The overall shape of the Twelve Steps is an arc from
sickness to health, the shape of the healing process itself. As
we follow that path our dreams can be a major ally to keep
us oriented and aware of when our addictions are winning
and when we are, of how far we have come and how far we
have to go. No matter how confused and caught up in the
effort we may be, our dreams offer us a unique way to keep
track of the progress of our recovery from within.

STEP ONE

"We admitted we were powerless over alcohol—that our lives had become unmanageable."

Before we finally admitted we were powerless over our addictions and intoxications and got into recovery, there was only one part of ourselves that wasn't pretending they didn't exist. That was our dreams. Looking back at the dreams we could remember from before recovery, they were a threat. They kept screaming at us (along with well-meaning friends, co-workers and loved ones), but we ignored them all.

Dreams, it turns out, cannot lie. Astoundingly, they also seem to be able to answer the big, overriding question that constantly baffles all of us, even those of us with years in recovery: How much is enough? We just don't know. But they do. Even in all the chaos and destruction we created, they always did. In Step One, we finally have to face the reality of how much addictive behavior is enough.

How does the mind create a dream? The raw materials are everything we have stored in memory, all the environments, the people, the thoughts, the experiences, and the feelings we have had in a lifetime. These elements are selected and organized with dazzling speed by the brain into something we have never encountered before and then presented to us during sleep.

Dreams represent a sizeable investment of the body's energies. As a matter of fact, the brain, only 2% of the body's size, uses about 20% of the energy we need each day. And the body is remarkably efficient. It does not waste resources.

So why does it produce a particular set of images? Why on one night and not another? The organizing principle seems to be intensity, just like our addictions. What makes a strong impression during our waking life (especially if it happens to involve all our cherished inner dramas and our fears) acts as a catalyst, a trigger for the dream to address. So, when in Step One we admit that our life has turned into its own kind of nightmare from which we cannot awake, we can expect our actual dreams to demand to be heard.

Nathan had a feisty little dream which shows how this business of dream-making works at the most basic level. It could easily be dismissed as a "snippet," short enough to be its own headline, but often these discarded little nuggets are doing their best to convey whole worlds of meaning. Here is the dream, with names changed, of course.

Dolores is wearing my gray t-shirt.

That is all there was to it.

We always have to look at a dream in the context of the dreamer's real life. Nathan was doing a serious and excruciatingly painful First Step around the debilitating sense of failure he carried around with him after decades of professional frustrations and defeats, even after many years in recovery.

Like all dreams this one existed in a timeless present, so, as always, it makes sense to tell it in the present tense in order to keep it fresh. Unlike longer, more complex dreams which can be somewhat dazzling and overwhelming, this one brought only two elements together and, rather than make an abstract statement about them, simply juxtaposed them, letting them play off against each other. This is a basic technique of the dreaming mind.

The dreamer explained that Dolores was a woman whose shares in meetings he had responded to deeply over the years. She was extremely warm and had a distinctively expressive voice. He always remembered what she said as she talked beautifully, and poignantly, about her travails in the world. He was always surprised and impressed that she could make herself so vulnerable.

Her promising career as a dancer ended in ruins; her subsequent jobs in the business world went nowhere; her attempts to get a higher education and her repeated defeats in trying to fulfill the math requirements were immensely painful for her; but she valiantly kept going and kept talking about what she was going through. This was only one part of her recovery story, but whenever she spoke about it he was amazed at her courage and identified with her completely.

The dream raised many, many questions. We discussed at some length what his beloved gray t-shirts meant to him. He loved the coziness of them next to his skin. They were modest and self-effacing. Easy to take care of. He didn't even have to think about them. He just took them out of the drawer and put them on. Actually they helped him to blend in, to feel like one of the guys.

We got as specific and detailed as we could about the actual reality of these objects in his life. And finally, why was Dolores wearing one of these gray t-shirts that he always wore peeking out at the neck of his comfortable, understated flannel work shirts? Eventually framing the question that way made the answer obvious. Enough pretending. Before the dream he couldn't see that his own pain, which he had been hiding (and hiding from) all his life, was right beneath the surface of his work life and that it showed through right at his throat (the place of speech) much more than he ever realized. He actually talked about and defined himself exactly the way Dolores did. His pain and sense of failure were just as tangible as hers were, but he didn't know it. In the dream she was telling his story, revealing how deeply crushed and on the defensive he was, for all to see.

The new information supplied by the dream was that his all-pervasive sense of worthlessness, which he wore like a second skin, was obvious to everybody but him and probably was holding him back in the world much more than he guessed. His First Step was working. He got to see first-hand how powerless he was, to realize that his choices were being made by his secrets, not by him.

Now he could take action on the information in the dream. Eventually he looked directly at his failures, genuinely let some go, and, in one case, returned to a couple of unrealized creative projects from many years before and started working on them again. The message he put out about who he was began to shift. As he put it, he was ready to "shout into the void." Of course he had to do all the hard work involved, but the dream was there to make the process more conscious, a bit smoother—a helpful message from within.

One of the most reliable tools to use as a slogan with dreams is, "What is the new information?" We quickly learn that until we get an answer to that question, we are fooling ourselves. The dream is never content to rehash what we already know. Why would the mind go to all that trouble and expense of energy otherwise? Something needs to be revealed. We are working at the growing edge.

Specific images drawn from the vast storehouse of our memories and experiences, a specific woman like Dolores or a gray t-shirt, are the building blocks of our dreams. The way the mind uses them is to assemble them into stories. These are the grammar, the basic structure with which the mind expresses itself.

It is no coincidence that all the great spiritual movements of the world are built around stories, parables or epic tales. Similarly, it is no wonder that our Twelve Step literature, and certainly our meetings and personal interactions, are built on stories. They are the most fundamental way we know of to connect with others and with ourselves.

We are all hard wired so we know viscerally how to listen to and tell a story. We have been doing this since we sat around the fire recounting in proud detail our exploits at killing woolly mammoths and each other, or, even better, drawing our dreams of bountiful hunting on the walls of our caves. A story has an interesting beginning that gets our attention; then comes the middle where things get complicated; finally it has an end where, to our relief, everything comes together, sometimes happily, sometimes not. We know we have to pay rapt attention to all of it, every detail, for it to make any sense at all.

We already know how to listen to our dreams.

Those of us in Twelve Step Recovery are at a particular advantage because we can tune in to an endless supply of moving and revealing human stories whenever we want to, simply by going to meetings. We become accustomed to hearing people give voice to their inner lives and we know we don't have to panic no matter how open and challenging they get. We just have to stay present, keep our mouths shut for the most part, and give our full attention to the speaker in order to learn something that has the potential to help us both.

We also have the model for respectful listening that comes with sponsoring and being sponsored. (We often overlook just how extensive an education we get in recovery on how to keep things simple, how not to judge and how to keep an open mind.) Paying attention has become second nature to us.

We also know more about asking searching questions than we might realize. Each of the Twelve Steps is an invitation and a challenge to ask questions about ourselves and our view of reality.

For instance, in Step One, what are we admitting? Certainly, that we are addicts and that as a result our lives are a mess. But more deeply we are admitting that we have been trying to act as if the laws of cause and effect didn't apply to us. Did we think we could devote all our energies to drinking, eating (or not), spending, drugging, being important, controlling, having sex or gambling and that there would be no consequences? Really? Well there were.

What is so painful about this Step is having finally to question ourselves, to own up to the fact that we were acting like total idiots. What were we thinking? How could we get something so basic so wrong? Who in their right mind would try to live in a way that contradicts the lessons that every human baby learns in the first months of life, that actions in the physical world have direct and ultimately predictable results? Yet such is the power of addiction that we did exactly that. We lived our lives as though we could get away with ignoring reality itself.

We are a self-deceiving lot, so we learn that we have to keep questioning our stories again and again and again. And we realize we cannot come up with these questions on our own. We need guidance. We need other human beings to help us see where we have been deluding ourselves.

Here is a dream about questioning assumptions.

> *Michelle dreams she is flying, as she frequently does in dreams. She is skimming over an embankment looking down on a young man struggling to mow the grass on it. When she gets to a nearby road she sees her mother and brothers in a car they actually own, an old Oldsmobile convertible. As soon as she catches sight of them she quickly comes down to earth before they can see what she is doing and express their disapproval of her as they have done all her life.*

Michelle was furious. Same old, same old. Even the same old *Old*smobile. (Dreams are full of jokes and puns, many of them quite clever and often quite revealing. There is something reassuring in knowing that the deepest, most unfathomable part of us, the level that creates dreams, has a sense of humor and of play.) She went on and on. This was yet another instance of the way they always "shot her down" and "took the wind out of her sails." She gave vent to her resentment and frustration with them. How often, she wondered, had their judgment of her spoiled her chances to express herself creatively, to take risks, to achieve the kind of success she desired more than anything else?

The dream confirmed the painful reality of her life. So what was the new information? The truth always feels new. This dream didn't. Not yet. There was literally something off kilter here. Anyone who has tried to cut grass on a steep slope knows how hard it is to do. It is exhausting and miserable work. Michelle skimmed over that and barely noticed the poor slob below her.

She was relatively new to A.A. and filled with the elation of new sobriety. This, she insisted, was the reason she had the dream. It showed how well she was doing, demonstrated her new freedom and proved that she could finally deal with her family in a mature new way.

There was one catch.

We seem to be able to do the most amazing and outlandish things in dreams. We live out our most exotic fantasies, we move back and forth in time without the slightest difficulty, and we fly effortlessly, soaring, gliding and gloriously defying gravity as if that is what we were always meant to do.

But only "as if." A large part of the thrill of flying in dreams comes from knowing we are getting away with something. We taste the euphoria of breaking the rules of being limited, earth-bound human beings. What we usually don't do, even in dreams, is assume that flying is a natural state. Everything in our being knows that isn't true.

No matter. Michelle was adamant. She never doubted she belonged in the air and was furious when she had to hide her flying from her family. It was her dream. No matter what anyone else might think about what was happening in the dream, ultimately she was the only one who experienced it directly and she had to be acknowledged as the ultimate expert, the final word. The rest of us were just observers.

Fortunately there is a way to cross-reference our understanding and to make sure that we haven't gotten sidetracked with all our questions. It is deceptively simple. At the end of the discussion it was time for Michelle to name the dream as quickly as she could without even thinking about it. This little trick serves to take us right to the heart of the matter, no matter how complicated the dream might be. (It also makes it easy to recall the dream in the future, complete with all the feelings and associations it brings up. Very useful.)

Michelle's answer just popped out and it stunned her. She instantly called the dream, "Getting High." She found herself suddenly admitting that, although she was feeling euphoric at her newfound sobriety, she was still acting like an addict, keeping secrets and denying reality. She suddenly got an inkling of the danger she was in. The dream didn't judge. It merely presented the reality of her situation.

As an addict she had long since lost the ability to trust her own instincts and behaviors when she was active, but the dream brought promising news. Somewhere within her a long-lost intuition was still alive and finding a voice, however fleeting. This new voice was grounded in reality and she might learn to trust it. Who knows, someday it might show her how to live a life that could be manageable after all.

Actually our dreams are doing their own version of a First Step all the time. What can be disconcerting about them is how completely they are onto us. We can hide nothing. They recognize our addictive behaviors long before we are aware of them.

As those of us who kept records of our dreams in pre-recovery therapy can attest, the over-the-top addictive behaviors were everywhere. Sadly, both we and our therapists were looking for other dynamics, so typically the subject of obvious addiction in our dreams never came up.

Even well into recovery, Step One awakenings keep happening. After many years someone will make the connection for the very first time that their substance of choice was what landed them in the gutter. It never occurred to them before. Similarly, someone else will blurt out that they finally can see how the chaotic world they grew up in is the reason they are having trouble connecting with people in their current life. Until this moment they had no idea of what was holding them back. The only thing worse than our problems is using our addictions to solve them.

Consciousness can be painfully slow at catching up to the awarenesses in dreams, but we can trust that without a doubt our dreams have been busy all along urging us to make connections, to finally accept the obvious, to bow to the inevitability of cause and effect. The sense of relief is profound, and so is the sorrow at how long we spent lost and desperate for help.

STEP TWO

"Came to believe that a power greater than ourselves could restore us to sanity."

What is sanity? Perhaps the best definition is a child being held tenderly—sanity for the child and for the adult doing the holding. (No wonder all those serene Madonnas have been so popular for so many centuries in Christian art.) One trait that many of us share as addicts is that we never learned how to soothe ourselves. "Restless, irritable and discontent," and proud of it. How often have we heard in the rooms some version of "I wanted to crawl out of my own skin?" We went to extraordinary lengths to get out of ourselves, sometimes with substances, sometimes with obsessions and sometimes by crawling into other people's lives instead of our own. The result was always the same.

For many of us, the first time we encounter a force capable of embracing us is a Twelve Step fellowship. It may be imperfect and we may struggle and resist, but it may be the first reminder we have as adults of what long-forgotten sanity could look and feel like. Deep, deep down we have just wanted to be left alone. The process of taking in the program can be daunting and slow, any belief that it could apply to us sorely tested, but our resistance as we keep coming back begins to dissolve.

21

Often our first "return" to sanity shows up in our dreams when we are feeling at our craziest. There they are with quiet, easily ignored alternative messages. Perhaps someone we know from the rooms shows up. Sometimes as we are faced with a challenge we think of a slogan or a snippet of prayer to help us out. Where did that come from? Something has shifted in us at a level far below our conscious awareness.

Clive was a young, prematurely gray graphic designer recovering from a cocaine addiction who shared with great feeling this dream where his worst fears had come true.

> *He has finally been "caught" for some unspecific, but heinous crime from his past. A young police officer comes to get him to take him off to prison for the rest of his life. The sentence passed on him is deserved, but what makes it particularly monstrous for him is that he will never be allowed to do his creative work again. The thought is so intolerable to him that he would rather die than go to prison under these conditions.*

He woke in a full-blown panic and even in telling the dream he was taut with fright.

We talked about the way he had lived his life as if condemned by some impending doom and spent a lot of time discussing his relationship with an angry, alcoholic father who had given him ample reason to feel that way. We reached a turning point with the dream when he was prompted to describe what the young police officer looked like. At first he had no real image of the man but on reflection he realized that he was dark-haired and in his mid-twenties. Suddenly he collapsed into himself. There was a long intense pause and eventually, in a strangled voice, he said, "It was me."

In that moment his whole being seemed to change. His hands relaxed, his face opened and his whole body unfurled.

Clive had condemned himself to a life-sentence of drugging, starving his creativity and trying to escape his ruthless inner policeman. Once he saw the pattern that had been controlling him for years he got the chance, for the first time, to be free, to step out of it if he chose. He named the dream, "I'm the Cop."

It is no surprise that the children of parents who were addicts have a lifetime of dreams involving Nazis, prison guards and torturers. All have been maimed and brutalized by addiction. But that is about "the other."

The true insanity is not to recognize that we have taken that cruelty and turned it on ourselves. No more abusers required.

Whether the question in a dream is, "Who condemns me?" "Who is looking for forgiveness?" "Who needs to be loved?" the answer is always clear, always a shock, and always the same. It is always me. I am the one who needs to heal.

Sometimes we can be nudged toward sanity. Sometimes we need something more dramatic. That is where nightmares come in.

Laura was having dreams that were so invasive and menacing that she thought she was going crazy. Night after night her darkest fears were being played out and she was afraid to go to sleep, terrified of the horrors within her and desperate for relief. Here is an example.

> *A man crashes loudly through thick woods in the middle of the night and slashes his way into a tent*

where she is huddling in terror with an older woman friend from her program.

She woke once again convinced she was losing her mind. She kept repeating that the dreams brought up "every ugly issue inside of me." After all her hard work in recovery it seemed like total defeat to see that they still held her so tightly in their grip.

Usually the first question to ask would be what was going on in her waking life that could be triggering such a powerful reaction in her dreams. She shook her head blankly. She could come up with nothing. Even naming the dream "The Invasion" didn't stir any particular response in her.

There was one element in this and most of her other dreams that didn't quite fit. In each she was not alone and there were supportive figures around her. This did nothing to lessen the stark horror she was experiencing. But they were there.

Just as she was getting up to leave she stopped part way and slumped back down into her chair, thumping her head in disbelief. She had just made the connection. A few weeks before these dreams started she came home on a Friday evening excited about leaving the next morning on a two-week vacation. She found that her apartment had been broken into and the standard items, some electronics and some jewelry, had been taken. City life. Strictly routine. She called the police to report the theft and they made a note in their log. She called her insurance company and they told her that her deductible was too high to file a claim. Case closed, so she went to bed and left for vacation at the crack of dawn.

When she got back the theft was old news and she had "forgotten" about it. Looking back, she realized that she had not mentioned the break-in to a single person in her life. The only people she had spoken to about it were the desk officer and the insurance adjuster. No wonder "her issues" had been triggered. She had been violated and was keeping it a secret, even from herself.

Not all nightmares are so easy to trace to their source. Laura just needed to acknowledge and come to terms with one particular loss, not the losses of a lifetime. For her the upsetting dreams stopped and she was finally able to get some rest.

For those of us who have strayed a long way from sanity, our programs and our dreams have a much slower and more demanding task. They are a part of us that will not give up, a fierce part of us that has a passionate concern for our well-being. If shocking, scary images are what are required to get our attention, our dreams will produce them. Gutsy and opinionated, at times they may feel like the enemies of sanity and recovery, but over time we can begin to see how deeply supportive they are. Ultimately we will come to realize that, above all, our dreams are kind.

Eventually as we recover we watch them settle down. The drama lessens. The dreams relax and become gentler as our lives do.

One young couple, Susan and Jeff, decided to stop drinking and to go into A.A. at the same time. They both experienced the classic symptoms of early sobriety, but what she remembers most is bolting up after the first few nights of not drinking and shaking her husband awake. She was experiencing what she thought were horrifying hallucinations. He reassured her that these were just dreams. People had them all the time and they were considered perfectly normal. She was amazed. Her addiction had cut her off from them. Her dreaming mind and her addiction were at odds with each other. Which would win?

Thankfully, dreams are determined. This is particularly clear in the case when, sometimes over a period of years, we have what seems to be the same dream again and again. Sometimes they are benign, such as when we dream of being a student again and having to take an exam we are totally unprepared for. No matter how old we are, that feeling of being unprepared is universal. We go right back to being four, seven, fourteen, nineteen or twenty, whenever we were vulnerable and lost and forced to cope with a world we weren't quite prepared for. The dreams don't let us ignore the fact that, no matter how old and experienced we are, some days we are just confused kids. Somehow that reminder can be immensely comforting.

Sometimes repeated dreams are much more freighted with meaning. Gavin had worked as a lawyer in very demanding, high prestige law firms until he was summarily fired. His mental health and untreated issues with addiction brought him down cruelly and swiftly. He was devastated and suicidal. The Twelve Steps, medication and intensive therapy (along with the unwavering love and support of a dedicated spouse) were what kept him from killing himself and eventually brought him back into life. A version of the same dream haunted him for years. He called this one "Always Rejected."

> *Gavin is at his first law firm, which we will call Partner, Partner and Partner, and is sitting at his desk. He knows he is no longer an employee and he fears he may not get paid. His boss has just nastily rejected a creative new argument that he has presented*

for a case. He sits there, stunned, not knowing what
to do.

Gavin, this brilliant, accomplished man, with his Ivy
League education had suffered the indignity of losing his
place in the world he created for himself. His intelligence, his
creativity, his warmth, compassion and humanity seemed to
count for nothing. What he was confronting was grief, the
grief that comes to all of us when we admit our
powerlessness. We negotiate, we deny, we rage, we hate how
much time it takes to fully feel and accept what our lives have
become. But we can follow our progress. Eventually, if we
look closely at each of our seemingly identical dreams,
especially if we write them down, we come to see that they
are not exactly the same each time.

In the first dreams he had after he was fired he was still
an active participant in the day-to-day workflow at Partner,
Partner and Partner. Slowly things shifted. (The dream above
happened about five or six years after leaving his law
practice.) In later dreams he no longer had an office, the
people he worked for were no longer there or were toiling
away behind closed doors. After about ten years the series of
dreams slowed down, but never stopped completely. Often
a rejection or a failure in the outside world can still have him
back at Partner, Partner and Partner, stunned and
heartbroken all over again.

What he does get back over time is the energy that was
syphoned off from him in having to deal with his grief. Very
often with someone just starting to pay attention to their
dreams, the first subject that comes up is not a present-day
event but the unmourned or unacknowledged death of a
beloved person or pet, sometimes decades after the loss but

as fresh as if it were yesterday. This is where sanity begins for them.

Drinking, drugging or acting-out dreams are another version of the same process. They have a huge emotional charge, and they can be terrifying. Am I at a new place in my recovery? Or am I about to relapse?

Whichever they are, it is important to talk about them with somebody else, preferably right away. Too much is at stake to ignore them.

> *David is at a wedding. He is in the wedding party and knows he has to give a toast to the young couple. There is an open bar. He is there getting his date a gin and tonic. The bar is lined with shots. He knows in the dream that he has over two years of sobriety, but he thinks that he could just quickly pick one up and knock it back and no one would notice.*

He woke up in a panic. Did he drink the drink or not? Had he lost his sobriety? He could almost taste the liquor on his tongue. Fortunately the first thing he did was call his sponsor.

The first thing she did was reassure him that taking a drink in a dream did not count as a slip. It counted as a reminder of the knife-edge of addiction. Each day is a reprieve. She pointed out that he hadn't actually taken a drink. He hadn't forgotten that he was in recovery. In the dream he was in a slippery and extremely stressful, alcohol-fueled situation. On top of that, he knew he had to give a wedding speech, a notorious set-up for public disaster. His sobriety was being put to the test in a variety of new ways. It was no surprise that the old sneaky ways of addiction would pop into his head.

It was probably time to look at his sobriety, to examine his motives. Was he becoming cocky? Were little dishonesties starting to creep into his daily life? Was stress, or success, getting to him, giving him an excuse to justify slacking up on his program? Was he acting impulsively? What major risks had he taken recently, ignoring the impact they might have had on him? The dream, which he called "Wedding Shots" was beautifully ambiguous. It challenged him to look at the way he was living with fresh eyes, always keeping in mind that a slip might be closer than he thought.

Charlotte also had a series of three "drunk dreams" that appeared similar on the surface but that had a different tone. When she had them she had been travelling for an extended period and was unable to get to meetings. The first she called, "None of Her Business."

> *A woman comes up to Charlotte and accuses her of drinking. She denies it vehemently even though she actually has been. Charlotte is upset that if she admits what she has done she will have to start her day count all over again. She is miffed.*

These dreams were a clear warning that at the very least she had to get back to meetings. She was at risk and she would ignore them at her peril. Her whole reaction in the dreams is dishonest and self-centered. She is much closer to actually drinking than she consciously realizes. These dreams are not a judgment. Rather they are a very loud alarm bell. She has been away from her program for too long.

If David or Charlotte had not paid attention to these dreams and then relapsed they would say, and believe, that it "just happened," it came from nowhere, out of the blue. We are all hugely impressed by the immensity and power of our own addictions. After all they speak to us in our own voices. We experience them as the worst, most devastating things that could happen to anybody, so we are somewhat disappointed to even consider that our dreams could give us a handle on them. As long as we don't numb ourselves with our substances or behaviors of choice, we can observe our addictions at work in us—threatening, bluffing, tricking, retreating, shape-shifting, lashing out, and finally collapsing in defeat. We are designed for awareness. Our inner drive for sanity is stronger than they are. We have a chance.

STEP THREE

"Made a decision to turn our will and our lives over to the care of God <u>as we understood Him</u>."

What would it feel like to be taken care of, even for a moment? Probably pretty uncomfortable. After a lifetime of figuring things out and taking care of ourselves, allowing ourselves to be taken care of takes a lot of effort. We have to decide to let it happen over and over again. Even if we have made a mess of our lives and acted like a bunch of arrogant, entitled jerks, the resistance to the whole idea is overwhelming. Do we dare let down our guard and stop fighting for one nanosecond? Too risky.

This was the dilemma Carol faced. After several years of hard work in her Twelve Step programs, she was testing the waters at getting into a new romantic relationship, her first since she had been in recovery.

> *She is working feverishly to drag everything out of a musty, crowded attic. The person she is doing it with is the former partner of her new love interest. They haul furniture and boxes down to the living room and they do the job with such single-mindedness and speed that soon they have trouble finding places to put everything.*

31

> *In the midst of all their activity, she notices that*
> *the fireplace in the room is just a mantelpiece pulled*
> *out from the wall a foot or so, and not attached to*
> *anything. To her surprise and alarm, as part of their*
> *task the two women break up some of the chairs and*
> *tables from the attic into kindling and use some of the*
> *old files and newspapers they find there to set a fire*
> *under a park bench in the center of the room.*

Something was seriously wrong. Fires belong in fireplaces with chimneys attached to clear away the smoke, not where people are intended to sit down together. She definitely made sure nobody would be making out on the park bench in the middle of the room anytime soon. Everything was inside-out or outside-in.

And why the frenzy? Why was she compulsively pulling out everything from the old, failed relationship and cluttering up the present with it? What was she doing teaming up with her new partner's ex anyway? Why was she torching her chances for a relationship and filling her life with thick, toxic smoke?

We can all look back and see times when we have sabotaged ourselves, but how often do we get the chance to watch ourselves in the act? Carol got to observe her self-will at work. She was, with great energy and determination, undermining any possibility of love and connection for herself.

She called the dream, "The Park Bench," a sad and wistful title. She could see the irony of romance made impossible, but what were her options? In the dream she didn't seem to have any.

This is when Carol took a pause. She spent some time talking with some of her program friends about the dream.

She sat with it, looking for a way through the impasse. Eventually she made a conscious decision to stop trying to impose her driving will on everything and everyone around her, to let the Gods smile on her if they wanted to. She decided to let her new relationship have a chance to develop as it was meant to without putting all her energy into destroying it.

The results surprised her. Her new love interest was an almost non-existent background presence in the dream. Now she could put her energy into finding out who her new partner actually was, and whether they were right for each other after all. It turned out they were and Carol's decision turned out to be life-changing and life-giving for both of them.

Carol decided to allow herself to be taken care of—but by what? She had no idea. Each time in the future she decided once again to cooperate with this unknown benign force, she began to develop a clearer and clearer picture of it for herself. She could not explain it to anyone else, but she knew she had tested it and slowly she came to rely on it in her daily decision-making.

A process like this was absolutely foreign to Eric, a gruff, no-nonsense therapist. In his early life, in the nineteen-sixties and -seventies, he had embraced a life of raw and unbridled drug use. Nothing could stop him. Many times he was there with his buddies as they died from exactly the same doses and combinations he was taking. He seemed invincible.

Somehow he survived this way for many years and finally managed to throw himself into recovery with the same fervor he had put into his drug use. He was able to develop his clinical practice, marry and have a family, but eventually a long and vivid series of dreams broke through his ordered existence. Night after night, week after week, a single wolf appeared in virtually every dream.

At first the animal simply showed up and stood silently on the periphery of his dream. Later it began to approach the dreamer and to make gestures for him to follow, staring at him with knowing, unfathomable eyes. As the weeks went by the wolf performed a number of feats that seemed to be ways of ingratiating itself with the dreamer. Then the dreams got even more challenging.

> *The wolf stands at the entrance to a cave in which an infant boy, perhaps the dreamer's son, is hidden. The wolf is on guard and moves aside obediently when the dreamer gets up enough courage to go to the child.*

In all the dreams the wolf's steady, powerful concentration never wavers. It seems intent on being understood.

> *Toward the end of the sequence of dreams the wolf comes right up to the dreamer and, taking the man's wrist gently and firmly between his teeth, tries to lead him along a path to a series of hills. The dreamer will have none of it and beats the animal off, bloodying its head with a flashlight. Still the wolf persists, trying to get behind him to nudge him along. When that doesn't work, the wolf runs ahead to a knoll, standing silhouetted against the skyline. Then he lopes back in an attempt to coax the dreamer to follow. Still, filled with dread and mistrust, the dreamer staunchly refuses.*

The silent intensity of the wolf was mesmerizing. This image would not be denied. The man knew the wolf and the wolf knew the man.

Eric was transported back to the raw, brutal years on the street in his drug addiction. He also remembered how seductive and treacherous he himself had been. He was not going to be conned by some wild animal pretending to be tame. He smelled danger. He was back living with death.

He immediately spoke about how terrified he felt every day of the animal within him. In practical terms, he was afraid to exercise because he thought that if he dared to build on the brute energy that kept him alive in his addiction, it would take him over again. He could never let down his guard. He worked his Twelve Step program more as a defense against his physical self than as a way to find a measure of freedom. The only time he could relax was with his wife and children when he could let his playfulness and tenderness come out. Even then it was an anxious and fragile truce.

The wolf in him had saved his life and the wolf in him was his mortal enemy. The dreams captured the standoff perfectly. What was he to make of them?

When he talked about them in a group of other people in recovery he got a wide range of responses, some useful, some less so. Some people were charmed by the wolf and assumed it had turned into a version of Lassie. They urged the dreamer to let himself be cared for. For them the wolf/dog clearly meant no harm.

Some introduced the concept of "power animals" and their importance in Native American traditions. Maybe this was a modern example. Others stepped outside the dreams and looked at them as an example of "survivor guilt."

None of the ideas, while interesting, moved the discussion forward. We tossed around lots of generalized thoughts and theories, but eventually it became clear to all of us that none of us had much to add that would help Eric come to terms with the power and urgency of his dreams. He desperately wanted relief.

One person had a specific contribution to make to our discussion. He pointed out that the history of actual interactions between man and wolf is much more complicated than we first realize. In spite of our fear of them, man is actually the deadly predator who has wiped out entire wolf populations in many parts of the world.

He suggested that Eric needed to spend time with a real wolf if he was ever going to come to terms with the dreams. He could at the very least immerse himself in as many documentaries about wolves as he could find. Even better, he could find out if there was a wolf park near the city he lived in. There he could confront, not the idea of a wolf, but the real thing.

Eric felt he already had the experience of a direct encounter with an actual three-dimensional animal in his dreams. This was a living image. He could touch it, walk around it and feel its breath. (It was not the polite, literary image of a wolf to be found in poetry or works of fiction.) Still he warmed to the suggestion that he could learn more. So he went to local zoos and spent many hours watching, smelling, appreciating and looking boldly into the eyes of actual wolves. It became a kind of meditative practice for him.

Over time the dreams and their meaning changed for him. Eric started to face how cruelly and violently he had attacked the wolf in his dreams. The animal had never provoked him. This was all about his own fear.

He did some research and learned that indeed wolves from the wild cannot be domesticated. It took millennia for dogs to evolve from wolves. His dreams directly contradicted reality. So what was happening here? Something quite remarkable to say the least.

It was only when he started to think about the concept of "being domesticated" that the dreams opened up for him. What was truly remarkable, close to miraculous, was that all the Twelve Step work Eric had done had actually domesticated *him*, and he had been unable to see or believe it. He couldn't believe his own recovery. Against all odds, the wolf in him that he was attacking had actually been domesticated.

On some level we all dream for each other, so the message Eric got from his dreams actually applies to all of us; whenever we are deep in our addictive behaviors or substance abuse we are acting solely out of instincts, fears and a drive for self-preservation. We are being less than human. We are behaving like animals, dangerous ones. But we can be domesticated.

What moves us beyond our addictions is our ability to conceive of something bigger—some sort of concept of God. This is what makes us human. We can make a decision. Do we want to live as part of a pack of untamed individuals? Or do we want to live as part of a fellowship of people where warmth and caring are considered to be a birthright for each of us? Our choice.

Seen from this perspective, no wonder that there is so much talk of God in the Twelve Steps. How we each imagine the source of caring is up to us, but we need to acknowledge that, even if we reject talk of a God or Higher Power entirely, we still have to confront the idea in order to raise our sights above the level of predatory beasts.

Still, for those of us who have had a history of turning our will and our lives over to our addictions we need to show some discrimination in just who or what we trust. Is it just a better-disguised version of our own will where we and our needs are still the center of the show? Ellen had a very challenging dream about trust, which she called "The Guru."

When the dream opens Ellen is an attractive young boy who is part of the inner circle of a great guru, basking in the master's attentions as his most favored follower. Time passes and as the boy's youthful beauty fades the guru loses interest. Others come along to take his place and eventually the young man leaves the guru to make his own way in the world.

Wherever he goes, he carries with him a great yearning to please the guru, to live up to the promise he once felt in being chosen and special. His life's goal is to figure out how to attract the guru's attention and approval once again.

Eventually, he meets a young woman and she agrees to marry him. In order to make their marriage real, the young man realizes that he has to present his fiancée to the guru. The holy man is appearing at a huge rally in a stadium nearby. The young couple arrives, he on foot, she carried in a sedan chair. They are immediately buffeted by the crowds but the young man, through sheer force of mission and determination, pushes and shouts his way through the mobs and finally past the rings of guards until he is face to face with the great spiritual leader.

Here the action of the dream both stops and speeds up at the same time. It all happens in a blur of silence. Before the young man can say anything their eyes meet. The guru shows no sign of having the

*remotest idea of who he is. They look at each other
for a fraction of a second as if from a vast distance.*

*At exactly the same moment the guru signals to
his "handlers" that it is time to leave and instantly
he is whisked away by a small army of bodyguards.*

*The young man is left stunned and confused. At
the end of the dream he stands immobilized, blinking
vacantly at the place where the great man had been
just a second before.*

There had been many gurus in Ellen's life, people
completely self-absorbed and incapable of ever seeing her,
let alone caring for her. Food was the false God she turned
to for comfort and it came close to killing her. Like her future
partner in the dream who was carried in a sedan chair and
whose feet never touched the ground, any contact with
reality was too painful to bear.

Ellen was stuck, the vital young male energy that she had
relied on up to now, gone. How could she ever conceive of
a kind, loving God who would offer her what humans clearly
could not?

For Ellen, the dream was an emotional "bottom." She
could see that she had created a false God, the guru, who ran
her life. After all her years in recovery, she was appalled to
see that she was still primarily interested in being desired,
winning approval from a world incapable of giving it to her,
living a life based on obsession and willpower alone. To her
horror she realized that everything was still about her, about
her determination to shape reality on her own terms. She was
devastated.

What was she to do?

Part of what intimidated her about the Third Step was
that she thought it said she would have to immediately come

up with a clear picture of what the God of her understanding looked like before she could proceed. That would not work for her and for many of us like her. Ellen read the Third Step again and realized that it asked her to make "a" decision, just one, to surrender to a new course of action, to not being in charge. Who knows. A whole new world might open if she did.

Maybe others already had a concept of a deity they could trust. She did not. So she decided that the best she could do was make a commitment to keep on going with the rest of the Twelve Steps. Like turning a huge ocean liner around, she would make one decision to surrender to whatever had kept her alive in spite of herself, followed by another decision, and another, in the belief that eventually they would put her on a course that was better than what she could come up with when left to her own devices.

She was surrounded by others in recovery who had taken this path and she saw that it seemed to work for them. The more they surrendered to recovery and the flow of life, the more they seemed to be taken care of. She watched them heal in ways she couldn't understand, so she made a decision to do the same. She had to give time for her understanding of the forces at work in her life to evolve at its own pace.

She also held on to the dream itself. It was a tangible reminder that some spark of life deep within in her was stubbornly fighting for her and that it had always been there keeping her best interests at heart.

STEP FOUR

"Made a searching and fearless moral inventory of ourselves."

An inventory is not a Russian novel, though many of us seem to think it is. It is a list. For those of us in recovery, since ours is a moral inventory, it is actually two lists—"What did I get right?" and "What did I get wrong?" (Our worth as human beings is not up for debate. That is a given, whatever we may or may not have done in the past and no matter how harshly we judge ourselves.)

A basic premise of recovery is that on some level we all know the difference between right and wrong, at least where our own actions and choices are concerned. We may not be aware of it in the heat of the moment, and certainly not in the fog and confusion of active addiction, but eventually when we stop and take a dispassionate look at the decisions we have made we start to get some clarity. Even at our worst, we always had some vague sense of when we were getting things right and when we were getting them wrong. Every time we tried to ignore this information, we just succeeded in making our lives more and more miserable.

If we have trouble getting honest with ourselves, one of Bill Wilson's greatest insights is that all we have to do is stop and look at our resentments. These are all the old, dead grievances we drag around with us and can't seem to shake loose. They keep reminding us of exactly what it is that bothers us most about who we have become. They are the truth-tellers, immensely painful, but ultimately they cannot be ignored.

The scariest part about getting started with an inventory is the fear we all share that deep down we are the one exception. We never really had any moral compass or, even worse, we have lost the right to be honest somewhere along the way—as if that somehow makes us special. Sheer arrogance. We are really not that unique.

Our dreams remind us on a daily basis that built into each of us is a place of searching, fearless questioning right at the growing edge of consciousness, a place that is incapable of telling anything but the truth. This is where we get to confront our most fundamental knowledge of right and wrong.

Mark was living a big, high-pressured life, but it had gotten really messy and complicated by the time he had the following dream:

> *Mark is on a battlefield in the American civil war. He is engaged in ferocious and bloody hand-to-hand fighting. His body strains as he lands blow after blow and he narrowly misses the deadly swings of slashing bayonets. Bullets and cannon balls are flying everywhere. Soldiers are dragged off horses as they crash to the ground and the whole scene is mired in mud and gore. The din is almost intolerable. There is even a space alien who shows up in the writhing tangle of battle.*
>
> *Suddenly someone shouts "Cut" above the racket and immediately all the combatants stop what they are doing and walk quietly off the battlefield*

together. Mark is at first bewildered and doesn't know quite what he should do, but he follows along. They all go backstage behind what turns out to be some very realistic scenery where they wearily put down their weapons and take off their tattered uniforms. To his amazement he discovers that this pitched battle is taking place on a giant sound stage and is part of a movie with an enormous budget, more than anyone has ever spent before. It is all part of a series of Super Star Wars blockbusters.

What he finds incredible is the life going on behind the scenes. There are long tables laid out with delicious-looking food of every description for actors and crew. Nearby there is an area for day-care and the actors and actresses mingle happily with their children between takes. Not far away is a place set up for people to work on an AIDS quilt. Here behind the scenes a warm, nurturing community life is going on. There are workshops where beautiful and useful goods are being made. Even the neatly tended cemetery to one side seems to fit into the picture of a town that is complete in itself. Everyone is very professional when they are in their roles as cast and crew, but they have this whole world in the background to depend on.

Mark wanders around this comfortable, supportive place, surprised by the intensity of his emotional reaction to it and scarcely able to believe it is there. As he drinks in the warmth and calm he finds wherever he looks, he is struck that this is much more remarkable than the make-believe world that was being created for the movie.

Doing an inventory invites us to shout "Cut" above the din of our daily lives. They seem so all-consuming, but until we stop and take stock we have no idea what is really going on. For a few days after the dream Mark felt a sense of quiet exhilaration, but he was soon back to being obsessed with all the turmoil around him, with who was doing what to whom. The dream, which he named "The Big Picture," still nagged at him.

What was he getting right and what was he getting wrong? For one thing, the dream didn't take Mark and his fancy, chaotic life as seriously as he did. What seemed to him like mortal combat wasn't real. Nobody was actually dying. Everyone was posturing, playing a part. Why was he letting it consume him?

He was making other dubious assumptions as well. His movie had to be the biggest blockbuster of all time. Really? We all live in our own movies. What did it say about him that his had to be so outsized? This was his addict's mind at work.

When he went behind the scenes he got very sentimental about this world of human values. He wandered around backstage being choked up and impressed, but always stayed an observer. He had been fully engaged in the staged battle, but here he stayed aloof. And his own values? What had happened to his connection with them? If he was in his addiction, did he still have any? How long was he going to keep distracting himself from his own humanity?

The dream was clear-eyed and firm. Mark had to admit it gave him an unwelcome new perspective on the way he was living his life. His actions and his inner nature didn't connect.

He didn't like the information in the dream. It was disturbing and he didn't know what to do with it yet, but he knew he needed to pay attention. This is how an inventory works. It takes stock but doesn't offer solutions. These would come as he took the Steps to follow.

Although he labeled his dream "The Big Picture," it also was a reminder of how limited our perceptions actually are. We think we know the big picture but we never do. Not ever. As addicts we think that the huge windowless sound stages of our minds are reality, but they are not. We need to get out into the fresh air from time to time. Mark's attention-grabbing dream gave him a tiny, but potentially life-saving glimpse of a much larger world, one actually worth inhabiting.

Ann had climbed the ranks of the corporate world and she too was restless and dissatisfied with the way her life was unfolding. She had a very different kind of wake-up dream, one that got her thinking about her choices and values as well.

> *Ann is looking out the window of the comfortable room where several of us meet to discuss our dreams. It opens to a small, leafy walled garden. Here she watches with horror as a blond, curly-haired eight-year-old girl is surrounded by a half-dozen swans. In utter silence the birds overpower the child, pecking and tearing viciously at her with their blunt bills again and again and again, until she sinks to the ground, no longer visible beneath their sleek white bodies.*

Ann shuddered visibly as she imagined the pain of being ripped at by those snub-nosed beaks. She knew instantly that all these swans were female and recognized immediately that she was a grown-up version of the little girl. The first thought she had was of her gracious, perfectly groomed colleagues at work. She felt isolated and undermined by them. None had become her friends. Her isolation was what made her feel suffocated and desperate to get out and start over somewhere else. She let herself realize for the first time how much she hated and resented them.

The dream, which she called "The Swans," seemed to give her permission to give voice to her frustrations, not just at work but in her personal life as well. She was not getting any younger and life seemed to be passing her by. She had made a huge compromise to devote so many years to her job in corporate training. It was an interesting field, bringing some humanity to the business world, but it hadn't gotten her anywhere. She always felt she was on the sidelines. And, once again, she found herself without a partner, living alone.

She had "worked" on herself for years, done all the right things, so why did she still feel as if she had gotten everything wrong? Maybe the swans were the clue.

The quickest way to do an inventory is to look at the four or five people we surround ourselves with every day. They are who we have attracted. They are an intimate mirror of who we are. (Just as the people around us in a bar or a club or other furtive places at 2:00 am on a Sunday morning showed us more about ourselves than we ever imagined.)

Ann attracted swans—cool, beautiful and inscrutable to humans. They float by on calm waters attracting admiration and awe. They are also silent. In the dream they are out of their element, on land and trapped in a walled garden. They have become deadly. Ann started to see that for most of her life she had tried to be a swan, beyond pain and vulnerability. She had always been so gracious, so appropriate, so kind. But she had been an enigma to herself and those around her. She could never let anybody know how fast and desperately she was paddling beneath the surface.

Her initial response to the dream was to claim victimhood and blame the women around her who behaved essentially the same way she did. That didn't work. The tightly controlled rules of behavior she had lived by without noticing had kept her isolated and unapproachable. She had to own just how much she had gotten wrong in her approach to life.

In the dream she was able to see all this from the comfort of a room filled with people in recovery. Without support and the previous Steps, it would have been too much to take in. It is not easy to look honestly at the choices we have made, choices that seemed completely natural and inevitable, but that are still killing us.

The action to take at this stage is to be courageous and sit with what we see. It hurts. We are always trying to escape the pain by getting ahead of ourselves, demanding that we see patterns before we even have a picture. The structure of the Steps is that answers will come, but just not yet.

Like it or not, no inventory of a life can avoid the subject of our parents, whatever role they took, or didn't take, in our lives. What did we learn from them that shaped our values, our ideas of right and wrong? A young woman named Helen brought one such dream to a group of us for discussion. It was quite short, but it struck a deep nerve in each of us.

> *Helen is running down a hallway, pursued by a shapeless black hole that threatens to draw her into oblivion. She is straining with all her might to reach her parents' bedroom.*

What made the dream so excruciating for her was that she came from a brutally abusive home, and to run to her parents' bedroom was to run toward a nightmare of violation and hurt. They had nothing to offer her, no guidance and certainly no comfort. She was alone facing the black hole of deadness and despair so familiar to any of us who have turned to addiction as a solution. Better to be drunk, or high, or dissociated, crazed by greediness or strung out on taking huge risks, numbed out on food or the lack of it, fixated on sex or self-harm, wired together by rigid self-entrapment—anything to avoid the all-consuming void.

Helen also realized that she was not a child in the dream. She was her current age and was still repeating the actions of a desperate child trying to get help from a place where she knew she could only be harmed. She had replaced her parents with her addictions. She knew she was making the wrong choice, but she continued to make it anyway. She called the dream, "No Escape."

The self-awareness in the dream was almost more than she could bear. Where was the moral choice, the chance to get something right? When faced with two impossible alternatives, what was she supposed to do? The answer was to stop running anywhere, to surrender. This would mean standing still, turning around and facing the fears and resentments that had pursued her all her life.

Her dream called for an act of great moral courage. She would have to trust that the Twelve Steps and the people around her would provide the container she needed, reminding her in Step Two that she *could* be restored to sanity, and in Step Three that she had decided to give up her way of doing things for something better, something new and as yet undefined.

Other people sitting in the same rooms with her had actually dared to make the same moral choice. She knew that. She could see that by staying with the Steps they had somehow found a way to live with the same inner contradictions and gut-wrenching emotional conflicts she had. In them she had a model for living other than the one she had gotten from her parents. Her fears weren't going to kill her. But running from them certainly could.

Before getting into recovery most of us had no idea that these moral conundrums were playing out in us day after day and it was inconceivable to most of us how intimately they were impacting our lives. Fortunately the natural process of dreaming is highly attuned to the myriad choices we make daily, sifting through the ones we can be comfortable with and the ones we can't. This is going on in us every night. When our addictions finally bring us to our knees, it can come as a surprise and a relief to find that our dreams have been doing an inventory for us all along and that they are always there to help us if we let them.

STEP FIVE

"Admitted to God, to ourselves and to another human being the exact nature of our wrongs."

Our addictions thrive on vagueness, the unasked question, the averted glance, the passive shrug. By doing our moral inventory we start getting some clarity on how we have lived, but what we end up with is actually a set of symptoms of something even more ominous going on behind the scenes. We are finally able to see how our addictions have taken over our lives. All along they have been defining us. Their history became our history. We disappeared. How did that happen?

No more. Now is the time for us to diagnose our own malady, to look at the exact nature of what we have been getting wrong. (It turns out to be just about everything.)

It is not enough to trot out the seemingly endless and shockingly cruel list of "negative-self" words with which we pepper our vocabulary: self-centered, self-loathing, self-deprecating, self-seeking, self-destructive, self-righteous, self-sabotaging, self-absorbed or just plain selfish. These are not particularly helpful in diagnosing our silent misery. They are just labels for the ways we have distorted ourselves. What are the treacherous, persistent thoughts underneath that have

51

made us so sick, stirred up so much chaos and robbed us of so much life?

One way to get to the core of our secretly held agendas and motivations is to try to summarize them in as few points as possible on a 3 x 5 card, as if we were going to do a quick, intense presentation to somebody on a short elevator ride. What really are our basic assumptions about ourselves and the world? What are the core beliefs that shape our daily lives? How did we lose track of who we are?

The first and most essential thing each and every one of us has gotten wrong is that we have underestimated the importance of honesty in our lives. Without it recovery is impossible. Without it we can never become people of character. It is at the heart of every Step and for all of us who slipped into addiction it was the first casualty.

After owning up to how dishonest we have been, we can begin to customize our own personal list of errors; but even then, when we compare notes with each other, it becomes clear that none of us is as unique and original as we thought. Many of the deeply held attitudes and habits of thinking that made our individual lives so intolerable fall into a set of common, predictable patterns.

A sample list of them might look something like this:

- all we have to rely on are our own minds and our ability to keep one step ahead of disaster, but we secretly have no idea how to deal with anything;
- we pretend we are just like everybody else, but deep down we can never forget that we are really worth less than nothing;

- the concept of love is nothing but a hoax, but we are desperate to be loved anyway;
- we hide the fact that we are greedy to win at all costs, and we need to use every trick in the book just to survive;
- our feelings and those of others are only useful as weapons, and fighting equals intimacy;
- the only way to protect ourselves in the world is to trust no one, risk nothing, expect nothing and judge everything;
- we are always right, so our job is to compulsively fix everything and everybody, except ourselves;
- the world and any deity that created it are terrifying;
- the cure for loneliness is isolation;
- when cornered, we can always inflict great cruelty on ourselves and others;
- life is meaningless and death is probably our only friend;
- we, and we alone, are "the exception"—and we are angry.

Imagine trying to create a tolerable life out of any or all of these beliefs—but that is exactly what we did, or tried to do. Fortunately we failed, and this is what brought us, at last, to the point of having to admit just what we had been doing to ourselves.

Please do not be misled by how stark and pared-down a list like this appears to be. Getting to our own version of it may be the most difficult and soul-searing thing that any of us ever have to do. Actually coming up with such a list for ourselves, taking it in, living with it, facing ourselves this honestly, even with the strongest possible support from others in recovery, doesn't make it any less daunting. At times it may seem like too big a challenge, too much reality, more than we can bear, but there is no way to avoid it if we want to move forward.

The exact nature of what Marilyn had gotten wrong in her life was screaming at her in a dream she took a particular loathing to. It was about a gerbil.

She was a dynamic, charismatic woman who was a brilliantly gifted teacher and educator. She had just returned from consulting with a school in an area of her city where people's lives had been devastated by a brutal attack that killed many students and several staff members, leaving the community exposed to fears of an endless nightmare of brutality and violence swirling around them. She had drawn from deep within herself, from her years of recovery and from her vast professional experience to offer what wisdom and support she could. She came away completely drained and sickened by what she had seen, filled with despair that the children and families would ever be able to survive emotionally from the horrors they had experienced.

> *Marilyn is sitting at a huge conference table surrounded by many of the distinguished professors and mentors from her past in a kind of Board of Directors meeting. Sitting beside her, directly to her right, is a human-sized gerbil. As the meeting progresses, she notices a small, normal-size gerbil scampering along the baseboard. Suddenly, as the whole assembly watches in a stunned and horrified silence, the big gerbil leaps from its chair, grabs the little one and, in the blink of an eye, gobbles it up in one bite.*

Marilyn certainly hated that gerbil. She went on at some length about the cruelty and unfairness of life. Her experiences in the aftermath of such mindless killing had shaken her to the core. She was morally, politically and socially outraged, exhausted and raw. (She named the dream "The Gerbil" with a dismissive wave of her hand.)

Sometimes it takes a shock to the system to make us realize just who exactly we are, just what exactly we have been getting wrong. The result this time was that, besides stirring up a rich combination of themes around mortality and powerlessness, the dream exposed what Marilyn's personal inner Board of Directors really looked like. It was obviously not up to the task of dealing with anything, let alone a serious crisis. For all the academic decorum of the meeting, sitting to her right in the position of power was a ridiculous, preposterous, out-sized, out-of-place gerbil, something she made very clear she completely despised. She was treating it as her most trusted human advisor, but to make matters worse, it was doing what gerbils have a tendency to do, eating other gerbils. (Who had she been devouring without realizing it?)

What she was particularly incensed about was that all the brainpower in that room was useless to do anything about the situation.

Going through the list of what we as addicts tend to get wrong, several categories would have been useful for Marilyn to look at—blind trust in the power of our intellects, a tendency to treat parts of ourselves with intense disgust, a need to judge everything around us and in us, a distorted sense of who or what to trust, denial of the primal messy parts of ourselves. How had she been able to function without recognizing all the conflicting forces within her? Somehow she had, but the time had come to confront all her secretly held beliefs and behaviors. They had been shaping her reality without her knowing it.

The trouble is that, even with the best of intentions, when we try to look at ourselves from a single point of view our self-protecting addictions always defeat us. If we are ever to address and hold in our minds something as important as the exact nature of what we have been getting wrong, we have to do so from many perspectives.

First, from the point of view of whatever being created us, can we admit what we have done with the life we have been given? In our own eyes, can we articulate who we have become? And reflected in the eyes of another human being, what do we have to say about our time on earth? If we ever hope to get free of the mind-set that has been controlling us we have to be as precise, brief and focused as possible.

This is very, very hard. But it is what we have to do if we want healing and relief. Above all we have to be especially careful about how and to whom we admit such a welter of deeply held information about ourselves.

Peter, who was doing another Fifth Step after many years in his program, decided that he wanted to find a professional to help him sort it out. The person recommended to him was a highly praised counselor who reminded him of Amelia Earhart. The night after he met with her for the first time he had the following dream which he named after the legendary aviator:

> *Peter is on a broad savannah. In front of him is a gorgeous vintage bi-plane, in mint condition. He is struck by the luscious beige/pink color of the leather upholstery. There are storm clouds approaching across the grassland. As he stands there, a rich, male voice tells him to get down on the ground and stay there.*

He ignored the message of the voice speaking directly to him in the dream and made another appointment to see her. She told him the dream was about his inability to trust, something she would help him work through. His next dreams were about television sets that worked on different systems, but that she explained as further evidence of his resistance. Eventually she told him she didn't trust his dreams because there was too much light in them. Where, she asked, was the pathology? What she couldn't see was the health.

He was being protected by his dreams and that straightforward, disembodied voice across the savannah. They were working overtime to make it clear that she was not the right person to work with, but they also gave him a glimpse at how his years in recovery were paying off. The very things about the dreams that made her nervous, his inner awareness and healthy instincts, were proof that he had been healing deep within without realizing it.

Peter's dream makes it clear how vulnerable we all are when we consider exposing and owning the exact nature of our illness. This is not what we traditionally think of as a confession where we tell an authority figure the worst things we have done in our lives, with the expectation that he (and it is always a "he") will somehow relieve us of the emotional burden we have been carrying around.

For Peter all three elements had to be in place and working together—the intuitive, God's eye view of the situation, (the disembodied voice in the dream), his own clear perceptions of what was going on around him, and the necessary presence of an understanding witness to act as a stand-in for humanity in general, (someone, his dream insisted, who was worthy of his trust). Without all these perspectives in alignment, facing the exact nature of all we have gotten wrong in our lives would be intolerable. With them, we finally dare to look and to actually see how our addictions have been playing out in us.

Armed with our individual list of negative and despairing beliefs, we can begin to listen for a voice of our own, instead of the tired, familiar and deadly voice of disease. One word of caution, however. No matter how clear a picture we are able to get momentarily of the exact nature of the things we have gotten wrong, over time our perceptions will prove inadequate, because our addictions are going to continue to evolve, to morph into something we can't see and we definitely aren't expecting. This is where our dreams can be especially helpful.

Clare was a woman who had many, many years in recovery, and so she was particularly upset to have a series of repeated dreams that seemed to show how futile and frustrating all her efforts had been.

> *Clare meets a powerful warrior woman dressed in highly polished armor wielding a deadly sword. She knows instinctively how determined this woman is to kill her. Only after a long and bloody battle is she able to kill her attacker, although she is badly injured in the skirmish and comes out of it barely alive.*
>
> *The most disturbing part of the dream is that just as she vanquishes her attacker and is about to breathe a sigh of relief, the warrior woman springs ferociously to life ready to do battle again.*

Clare named the dream "Warrior Woman." For her this dangerous figure was all too familiar. It was her mother, her boss at work, the world in general. She was sick of the constant battle to survive against all of them. Was she doomed to keep up the fight forever?

Telling the dream at a meeting was her cry for help. She had lost patience with herself and was deeply frustrated with her recovery. Why, after all her years of hard work did nothing seem to have changed?

She had to admit that over time she found herself becoming hardened, trapped in her own armor, always ready for a fight. She knew that somehow her addiction was winning, but she couldn't figure out how.

Her addiction had changed and she hadn't. In fact over time she had become more and more rigid, not less. The suppleness with which she had once been able to come to terms with the things she had gotten wrong in her life was just a sweet memory. She knew she was at risk.

The dream pointed out that Clare's old thinking was back disguised as her own strength. She had reverted to being someone who was little more than the mirror of a hostile world. She was behaving reflexively, relying on her wits and her willpower to survive. She was so busy seeing herself as a victim that she could overlook how cold and steely her hand-forged defenses had become. Life was again a zero-sum game of kill or be killed. Her fear, which was really fear of who she had become, told her that she was on her own and defenseless, so she had to do whatever was necessary to protect herself. She also had a whole new set of reasons to judge herself, to blame herself for her lack of progress and to put herself down—and all this after many years of heartfelt dedication to her program.

Clare's basic beliefs about herself and the world, which had gotten her into trouble in the first place, were back in a different and very confusing form. Her warrior-like commitment to recovery had become her deadly enemy.

Our addictions are opportunistic and ruthless. Every time we confront them we find out, in no uncertain terms, that they have always been there—waiting, evolving. Any complacency in dealing with them can be deadly.

Fortunately the Steps can be just as patient, relentless, flexible and adaptable as our addictions are. Clare had done a Fifth Step early in recovery and she had experienced its power to get her unstuck and open a window of compassion on her struggles. It had been a great relief to acknowledge the exact nature of what she had gotten wrong in the past. It was time to for her to trust the open-hearted embrace of the program and come to terms with what exactly she was getting wrong now.

STEP SIX

"Were entirely ready to have God remove all these defects of character"

The worst part about seeing exactly what we have gotten wrong in our lives is that we can't stop seeing it. It is everywhere. It is so blatant, so obvious, so profoundly embarrassing. We can't stand it any more.

More galling yet, nothing has changed. We are no longer able to plead ignorance, yet we still find ourselves behaving exactly the same way we always did. Once again our best intentions to improve our character and our behavior don't work.

Finally we are ready for a big change, a complete overhaul in our approach to life. The problem is we can't do it ourselves. We have to wait for it to happen. We are at an inflection point.

The self-justification, manipulation and self-pity don't work any more. We are now undefended and vulnerable. Our addictions, the great love of our lives, have betrayed and abandoned us. The old endlessly complicated stories we told about ourselves ring increasingly hollow. We begin to see that our relentless habit of trying too hard and never allowing life to unfold naturally has taken a huge toll. Even our last go-to line of defense, lapsing into an all-too-familiar state of helplessness and confusion, falls flat.

We know from years of experience with addiction what it is like to feel stymied. This is different. This is the time for inaction with a purpose. No more distracting ourselves. We can't be the person we used to be and we don't know who we will become. This is a huge period of adjustment for us, so we need to give ourselves time to get ready for it. The best thing we can do is pause, pay attention, stay open and wait to see what happens.

As a woman with many years of recovery from an eating disorder, Janet was almost too familiar with this level of frustration. The particular cruelty of food addictions is that abstinence is not an option. Every day, several times a day, she had to confront the need to eat. Even in her dreams, she found no escape. Every night, every single dream had something to do with food. She tried to find just one that didn't, but she finally had to give up.

> *Janet is looking at a glistening white piece of Arctic Char on a plate. It is radiant, shimmering with purity and freshness. It is a special gift that has just been presented to her with great ceremony by a trusted neighbor and friend in recovery who has been to northern Canada and caught the fish herself. She then had it frozen, packed in ice and shipped home.*
>
> *Janet is touched that her friend would share such a delicacy with her and can only imagine how delicious it is going to taste.*
>
> *The trouble is that she doesn't know if it is safe to eat. How long before it could be frozen in the wilderness? Has it been handled carefully enough, kept at the right temperature in shipment? When did her friend thaw it out?*

To make matters worse she doesn't know how to cook it. What temperature will be high enough to kill any pathogens without destroying the texture and flavor? She knows it is a rare species that must not be overcooked or it becomes inedible. She has also just read that most fish in the Arctic have been contaminated with mercury.

She will have to tell her friend how it tasted, but how can she eat it? What will she say if she ends up throwing it away? If she does, will she have to lie?

She woke in turmoil. This riddle had no solution. What should she do? Her addiction was flaunting itself, taunting her, reveling in its ability to confuse, paralyze and humiliate her once again. She was convinced that she would always be defeated by food and her relationship to it and to make matters worse, she was particularly shaken by the idea that this woman and the Twelve Step program she was part of might be trying to destroy her. She felt that she had no options left, that she was right back to the depth of pain and paralysis that had brought her into recovery in the first place.

Never before in her life had her addiction revealed itself as clearly as in this dream. What was happening? The most likely possibility was that her addiction was under threat. This was its last stand. By doing her inventory and finding out exactly how her mind could be co-opted, she was now in a position to step back and observe her addiction in all its treachery and watch it thrash itself out.

She named the dream, "How Much Is Enough?" This is the basic question none of us knows how to answer and one we all have to sit with every day. How many precautions would be enough? How safe was her food? How much could she trust people in her program or even her own perceptions? The question of how much food was enough never came up. Her mind never let her get anywhere near cooking it or tasting it, let alone daring to enjoy it. She was actually starving.

How much more time was she willing to squander on her glittering addiction before it killed her? The answer was clear. She had had enough.

Being ready to let go of the old raging fears, doubts and confusions of the past without giving in to panic takes great courage and resolve. Will they drag us down again? In the middle two Steps of the Program we are encouraged to expect that all the distortions and accretions that come with years of living with addiction will be removed; then, once that has happened, whatever is holding us back from a full and healthy life will be removed as well. What would that look like? And is it even possible?

For Carlos the answer came in the form of a series of dreams that puzzled him deeply. They were long and apparently shapeless but here is the general outline, along with his reactions while they were taking place.

> *Carlos is at a seemingly endless reunion of people who have come together with the vague intention of putting on a conference in 90 days. They are part of a community. They have all known each other since childhood and are having a terrific time together. All their children and pets are there and the activities go on and on—all the things that people do, playing games, talking, eating, having fun.*
>
> *He walks through the crowd taking everything in. At one point a couple of older women wearing gorgeous patterned fabrics, like the fanciest clothes of his mother and his aunts, are having a noisy spat.*

He simply goes up to them, looks at them, says "Basta"—enough—and walks on. They settle down immediately, almost grateful for his intervention.

The dreams seem never to end. The pleasant activities go on unabated for hours, and the energy and good humor never let up. Eventually he starts to recognize that none of this is how he would really choose to live himself. He never wants to have a family, not even pets. He likes quieter, more private pursuits.

He is not inclined to be part of this slice of life, but to his great surprise he doesn't find himself judging these people or looking down on them either. He actually appreciates the beauty and richness of what is going on around him.

Carlos awoke from the third night of these dreams annoyed that he had wasted so much time on something so aimless. It was only when he came up with a name for them that he began to see what was going on. He called the dreams, "Ordinary People."

Before his recovery he would have judged these people ruthlessly. He wouldn't have tolerated being around them for a moment. Something in him had actually been removed. Gone was the judgment, the sense of being different, of being better—yet also the feeling of being a lonely outsider, not quite a member of the human race. If he had not identified these traits of character in his short list of the things he had gotten wrong in the past he would not even have noticed them missing. Now, without any effort on his part, at least for the moment, Carlos could see they were gone. Vanished.

He was blindsided by the change in himself. All those meetings he had gone to with their sense of community and connection had done something to him without his realizing it. Even the sly reference to a shared goal to create a result in 90 days made him chuckle; dreams have their own gentle humor.

The first symptom that an addiction is at work in us is the sensation that we are somehow exceptional and special, even if it means telling ourselves that we are exceptionally useless and dull. This is what makes us worthwhile and gives our lives value and meaning. The thought of being average or ordinary is too painful to contemplate. We do whatever it takes, no matter how desperate, in order to assert that our lives are worth something.

The big fear is that if we give up the heat and intensity of our addictive minds—the judgments, the cleverness, the dishonesty, the arrogance, the martyrdom—we will become passive, boring nobodies. The idea that we are at our essence just decent, kind human beings feels like a threat. We believe the hidden emotional lie that health and sanity are not our natural state.

The truth of the matter is just the opposite. What keeps us flat and one-dimensional is our addiction at work. As we allow it's grip to be lessened we find we actually have the chance to start to grow and become interesting human beings.

Most of us have a lot of catching up to do. We know on some level that we stopped developing and maturing when our addictive behaviors took us over—but we hung on at all costs, refusing all change. We missed so much.

That still doesn't mean that we don't grieve the loss of what we need to have removed or that the process is always easy. It is not.

Paul woke every morning of his life flailing in a pool of terror and anxiety. Again and again his worst fears came true. Devastating events kept happening and over the years he learned to cope with them by diligently applying his program of recovery. But this latest news was too much. He was diagnosed with advanced lung cancer. Even after he had major surgery he was given at best a 50/50 chance of survival. The medical protocol at the time was do nothing more and to wait to see whether the surgeons had been able to get everything. This kind of anxious waiting was exactly his worst nightmare.

An oncology nurse in his recovery program told him of a clinical trial of a form of chemotherapy approved for other cancers that was now being tested on the form of cancer he had. The idea of enrolling in such a long shot created even more turmoil and uncertainty for him, but in an act of desperation he signed up to take part anyway. Here is his dream.

> *Paul wakes up in a panic in an old New England house he has gutted and renovated right down to the laths in order to restore its former loveliness. He realizes that a flash fire has just raced through the building, charring everything. He dashes upstairs to the third floor and looks with horror at the ceiling of the attic where the chimney goes through the roof. Somebody has sealed it off with heavy metal plates so that a fire in any one of the elegant fireplaces below would create a disaster.*
>
> *Everything in the house has been singed. The accumulated dust and dirt of over a hundred and fifty years have gone up in smoke. In his words, the "detritus" has been "surgically removed." Some of it*

*is still smoldering, but the fire appears to be going out
on its own.*

*Paul rushes downstairs and tries to tell his
former wife what has happened, but he can't quite get
her attention. Sitting empty-eyed with her on the
stairway, he is the picture of a broken man.*

The last thing he needed was a scary dream on top of
everything he was going through. How could life be so cruel?
So this is what having everything removed felt like. Worse
than he had ever imagined. He certainly hadn't been ready
for this.

Paul called the dream "Gutted." For him it was the end
of hope. Nothing was left. But was that true? Although the
fire removed all the junk that had accumulated over the years,
there was still a stairway to sit on. The structure was still
sound. The classically handsome Greek Revival house of his
dream would still stand.

Until he discussed the dream with someone else, Paul
couldn't see it offered him a perfect image of the
chemotherapy at work in his body, a controlled conflagration
meant to wipe out everything in order to destroy the cancer.
He was amazed. The clear message of the dream was that the
treatment was going to work—and that proved to be true.

Not only was he being made whole on the physical level,
but the devastating grip of fear that had possessed him all his
life started to relent. His fears and anxieties didn't suddenly
disappear—far from it—but he could tell that something in
him was fundamentally changed. He no longer saw himself
living in a world of wanton cruelty where he could at any
moment be flicked away like an offending fly.

By capping the chimney in the dream, his doctors or
some force unknown to him had set up a situation where the

life-threatening panic occupying his inner life could be removed. The result was a new bedrock level of peacefulness he had not experienced before. He was now ready to live in a different way.

Brian glimpsed a similar shift in his life in one of the short, pithy dreams he typically had. (Our dreams are as individual in form and content as we are.)

> *Brian is standing in front of a large black and white photograph, which is also a mirror, but the whole scene has the feel of a black and white movie. At first the image/reflection he sees is greyed off and indistinct but gradually it becomes clearer. As he continues to look at it he suddenly realizes he is looking, maybe for the first time, at a clear image of himself. But then comes the shocker. He realizes he really, really likes what he sees.*

Enough of not looking. Enough of seeing himself through the veil of his addiction. Brian was ready to have the old filters removed. He named the dream, "Me."

He hadn't changed his perceptions. Somehow they had been changed.

Nothing had to be added. He didn't need to be improved. He was fine as he was. This came as a great revelation to Brian, and not one that he expected. To look at himself through accepting, even adoring eyes—the God's eye view—was quite unsettling for him. What was he supposed to do now? How was he to proceed? A great chasm opened before him. Everything seemed possible but he didn't know what help he needed in order to move forward. Turns out what he actually needed to do was *ask*.

STEP SEVEN

"Humbly asked Him to remove our shortcomings."

We spend a lot of time trying to define the word "humbly" as if we have never heard it before. Basically it means, be pleasant, be decent, be right-sized; but mostly, for those of us who are addicts, it means, "Don't be a jerk." Since we have all had the experience of being too self-involved and demanding for our own good, we really don't need the concept explained to us. What we are avoiding is the action-word it modifies, the verb, "ask."

What did we actually ask for today? Anything? Nothing? More of the same, or a chance to thrive? A small life, or the opportunity to grow and change, with all the discomfort that comes with it?

How are we protecting ourselves from living the fullest life possible? What are the human shortcomings, the blocks we are hiding behind and allowing to stand in our way? Clearly the big things we have gotten wrong are huge stumbling blocks and need to be removed; but so do many of the "little" habits and quirks of personality and ingrained attitudes that we barely think about. They get us in serious trouble again and again, and hold us back in ways we can hardly imagine. In spite of our best efforts, they stay just below our awareness, almost invisible. Many of them need to go too.

What would it be like to imagine a healthy life? Who would we be if we felt entirely comfortable inhabiting ourselves exactly as we are? How would we act? Where would we even begin? We begin by *asking*.

First we could ask for a day of fun, laughter and lightness of spirit. That would go a long way to setting the right tone. We could focus for a moment on the gift of life itself, on our recovery and our fledgling relationship with a power greater than ourselves. We might just find that a large dose of thankfulness is in order.

Then we could ask to be surrounded by love, warmth and kindness, and, even better, to be a source of love, warmth and kindness for those around us. We could ask for and actually notice the health, energy and vitality fueling us, whatever aches and pains and challenges we might be experiencing. A simple request to be kept safe in the world might be a good idea.

Have we paid attention to the opulence all around us, the fullness of life bursting out everywhere, almost too much to bear? The friendships, the human interactions, the beauty everywhere if we open our eyes to it. (We might even consider adding to it in some small way if we can.) We can look at the way money, resources and opportunity show up in our lives and ask to be able to be generous with what we have. The same goes for our talents, skills, abilities and experiences. How can we use them to create the most fulfilling, meaningful, successful lives possible for ourselves and others?

What is stopping us? What new ideas are out there? What can we learn or see in a new, creative way? How can we align our attitudes and actions with the world as we find it? We can ask to have an open heart, an open mind, and a self open to the reality within which we exist. Are we brave enough to invite life into our lives, to find a voice, to be seen, to dare let our spirits soar, knowing that the more we surrender the more we will be taken care of?

Do we dare to ask for every cell, organ and system in our bodies to be aligned with the force of life? Can we take a moment to be thrilled by consciousness? (It is shocking how much we take this utterly astounding, all pervasive, fact of our lives completely for granted.) Do we have the nerve to flirt with giant feelings of gratitude, reverence and awe?

These are all symptoms of a healthy life and the amazing thing is that if we don't ask for them we don't even notice we are getting them. Asking makes all the difference.

Richard asked to have the invisible obstacles that held him back from having a more satisfying relationship with the people around him removed. He was a well-respected and even revered teacher, but many of his pupils, in spite of his best intentions, found him distant and intimidating. He had the following dream that offered him insight into what was going on:

> Richard is in a town that is right out of an old movie western. The streets are unpaved and the sidewalks are made of wood. Somebody is lying in the street having a siesta.
>
> A little old madwoman in a bandana rushes out and pours cold water on the sleeping person. She has done this many times before, jealous that her victim had dared to have a love affair with someone in the past.
>
> Richard becomes furious and decides to act. He grabs the old woman and she becomes hysterical, screaming and fighting like a crazed animal. Hate wells up in him and he decides she needs to be

> *tortured. He holds fast and takes her into her room*
> *in a cheap modern hotel. He drags her into the shower*
> *and, keeping the shower curtain between them so she*
> *can't spit on him, turns on the coldest water possible.*
>
> *His intention is to torture her to death by*
> *alternating hot and cold. (He has a vague idea that*
> *this was a practice in Czechoslovakia under*
> *communist rule.)*
>
> *All of a sudden he pulls himself up short. He*
> *realizes that he can't go through with his plan, so he*
> *simply stops what he is doing and abruptly lets her*
> *go.*

Richard called the dream, "Coldness." He was not a cold man—anything but—but he saw immediately that, without realizing it, he instinctively put up an invisible shield of coldness to protect himself from everyone around him. It had given him a sense of safety in the midst of the turmoil and cruelty of his childhood, but it had taken on a life of its own. He wasn't aware of the message he was putting out in the world, but as he progressed in his recovery he got a stronger and stronger sense that something was amiss.

In the dream Richard got a chance to see the violence and rage fueling his behavior, and label it as the madness it was. He was shocked and appalled, particularly since he had always been terrified that, deep down, he was just as insane as his family had been. What he didn't realize at first was that in the dream he spontaneously made the decision to let the madness go. He was given the opportunity to watch himself change.

Only on reflection did he realize how much his desperate need to assert coldness had been a symptom of something greater, an assertion that he would not be defined by madness and hate, even though for years it had secretly robbed him of the depth and ease of connection he had always yearned for.

For Richard, this dream captured the moment of having a shortcoming removed. Shortcomings are not just the obvious defects of character we have identified, but anything we do to defeat ourselves from being the person we have the potential to be, the seemingly small ways we keep ourselves from flourishing.

Speaking of potential, now might be a good time to go back and think about the list we made of things we got right in our Fourth Step moral inventory. (Some of us may have overlooked that part completely.) Even in the depth of our addiction, we were more than the sum total of what we were getting wrong. We must have had something going for us or we wouldn't have survived. Maybe it came down to grit, sheer stubbornness, some kind of passion or simply our refusal to die but, whatever got us through, it turns out we always had greater inner resources than we realized. What is still keeping us from using them? What are our blind spots? What are the inner strengths that we need to build on in order to become the fullest possible version of ourselves?

The goal is not to reach some austere idea of perfection but to pay attention to our behaviors and their consequences. What we may dismiss as a pesky bad habit or a little quirk of personality may be more threatening than we want to admit. After all, our addictions are endlessly inventive. The sober alcoholic can find himself standing in front of the refrigerator eating ice cream by the gallon right from the container. The former cocaine addict can risk bankruptcy shopping endlessly for jewelry online that she doesn't want. The recovering sex addict can scarcely believe the violent outbursts of anger he is having on the subway. None of these behaviors are who we want to be. Our shortcomings humble us.

We may all need multiple programs but there is one common thread—our emptiness and our endless need for more. In recovery there is no small stuff, nothing too insignificant to ignore. Everything we do has an impact on who we are. The cleansing we ask for has to be as complete as possible—and we can take nothing for granted.

Even small victories shimmer. Lily had a sweet, mild-mannered dream that marked a real turning point for her.

> *Lily is with a man she has started dating and she is having a wonderful time with him. They are kissing and just enjoying being with each other. He offers her something to drink. It happens to be non-alcoholic but she realizes that she hasn't told him she is in recovery.*
>
> *For the first time ever she realizes that she can take her time and wait for the right moment to tell him that she is an alcoholic. There is no rush.*

For Lily the dream marked a huge shift in her thinking. She had spent her whole life urgently trying to explain herself, to make herself understood, because she believed that no one would ever understand or accept her, especially if she admitted she was an alcoholic. In the dream this life-long tendency had been removed and for the first time she experienced a sense of comfort in being exactly and fully who she was. She had come a long way from wanting to crawl out of her own skin.

Lily named the dream, "The Sober Drunk Dream." It was a perfect choice. She was not surprised at the idea of a relapse dream, but a dream about progress or about the absence of her old ways of reacting amazed her. In reality she had yearned for the change for a long time. She had asked for relief and waited. Had she done enough? Yes. That was the point.

John was also desperate for his life to change but he was not getting the results he longed for. He was struggling with a job search that had lasted for months and seemed to be getting nowhere. This was his dream.

> *John is on an Air France jet about to take off for Paris. As the plane lifts off the dark runway he notices the pilot standing on the ground just a few feet below it. The flight does not gain altitude and they end up crashing in slow motion through a rounded stone tunnel, breaking off the wings and leaving only the fuselage intact on the other side. The plane doesn't burst into flames when it skids to a halt, so all the passengers climb out, buoyant and relieved. John takes one of the two bottles of good white sparkling Bordeaux being passed around, pops it open and serves it to everyone. (He doesn't appear to be drinking.)*
>
> *He is concerned about arrangements for his connecting flights and focuses his attention on having them changed.*
>
> *The pilot, it turns out, is very old, going deaf and blind, but he loves to fly. He has devoted his life fully to it. The dream ends with some vague, but gentle thoughts of whether a class-action suit might be in order, or whether it might be better to overlook the old pilot's error and let him keep flying because it means so much to him.*

John's reaction to the dream was strange. One of his strongest desires was to take a trip to Paris. If he could only find a job maybe he would. He saw an easy parallel with the dream and his frustrated job search. He also had no difficulty seeing defects of character he had already identified in his moral inventory, his obsessive focus on others and his own inability to stand up for himself. He called the dream, "Clipping Our Wings," as if it was about a vaguely defined group of passengers and not about him. (This is why we tell our stories in the first person in recovery to remind ourselves that they are about our own healing, no one else's.)

In the dream he had nearly died and he apparently felt nothing. He trivialized the danger and quickly turned it into a social event, focused on his own little agenda and tried to dismiss any unpleasant repercussions. What was he thinking? What was wrong with him?

For one thing John had turned his life over to a pilot who was old, blind, deaf and earthbound, and who he wouldn't hold accountable. How many of us have saddled ourselves with an image of a Higher Power just like that? Unexamined, ineffectual and dangerously out of date. It can kill us. We deserve better than that.

Just like John's life force, the dream trails off into confusion and dangerous inaction. Passion can get us in a lot of trouble, but so can lack of passion, especially when we have to insist on our own safety or sell ourselves and get a job. John's dream is a reminder that what he is doing in recovery is serious business, life or death, and he can no longer afford to take it lightly. It takes great determination, and even a certain ruthlessness to get our lives back. Old reactions to pain—numbing out, ignoring, and belittling it—no longer work.

All of this inner struggle was completely invisible to John in his waking life. He had no idea how much passivity and superficiality defined him. But he could no longer dismiss them as little quirks of personality. He could see they were killing him. He had the option to ask to have these shortcomings removed and his passion for life restored.

It is one thing to take our recovery from addiction seriously; but quite another to be too serious about ourselves. That is the sign of another shortcoming altogether. Actually one of the surest signs that we have had something removed is that we start to see the humor in what we have been up to.

Barbara had been in recovery for a long time and had become quite formidable and set in her ways. This was her dream.

> *Barbara is in London visiting Buckingham Palace. She slips behind the guards and finds herself in Her Majesty's sitting room having tea. The two women get along famously and chatter on about the appropriate hair length for older women, (medium), opting not to have plastic surgery for the skin under their eyes, (it didn't work for Princess Margaret), being addressed familiarly, their roles in life, having mothers who drank, never wanting to retire, the right clothes to wear to a christening, (always fun events), not knowing what to make of their children, the pleasures of nearing the end of life, (the Queen thinks of it as a beginning).*
>
> *Barbara wakes up very irritated. She realizes that on virtually every subject she is more rigid, judgmental and arrogant in her attitudes than the Queen of England.*

Barbara's name for the dream made it clear what she needed to have removed. She named it simply, "Lighten Up."

STEP EIGHT

*"Made a list of all persons we had harmed, and became
willing to make amends to them all."*

After all this effort we have finally started to get ourselves
back. But now what? We wake up and find ourselves staring
at the wreckage everywhere around us. We can't avoid it. We
caused a lot of it. What happened, happened, and there is
nothing we can do to change it. A glum prospect.

In order to go on we have to find a way to clean up the
mess or our lives will be intolerable. Fortunately we have
already made mention of the collateral damage we caused to
people in our moral inventory, so we have a partial list of our
victims to build on. Now it is time to put these people front
and center, and pay full attention to the impact we had on
them.

In therapy the theory is to delve into the past in order to
find out who we are. In recovery we find out who we are in
order to come to terms with the past once and for all. One
approach doesn't exclude the other, and the two can work
well together, but in recovery we are faced with the
uncomfortable task of identifying "all persons we have
harmed." Who are these people, anyway?

81

Welcome to the new world of "otherness." It can be quite an exotic place for us. It can also be quite disorienting. For many of us it comes as something of an unpleasant surprise that there were actually other people out there at all—let alone that we had any impact on them. When we were in our addictions part of us thought we were invisible, outside of the world of cause and effect. Our self-centeredness kept us isolated and blind.

Other people? We tolerated them, but they didn't really matter. And that was all the permission we needed to treat them terribly, even though we thought we could trick them into believing we noticed them, even cared about them. We didn't. Our addictions always came first—not just the obvious destruction of our chemical dependencies and obsessive behaviors, but, lurking beneath them, our hidden need to control everything and everyone in our world. That drive in us has done a spectacular amount of damage to those around us, most of it hidden.

What does it mean to "harm" someone, anyway? What were the harms we did? A good place to start is by looking back at the list of "the exact nature" of the things we got wrong that we put together in the Fifth Step. Just as a reminder, this is who we were. This was the playbook we used. We were nuts. It is no excuse, but we were completely in thrall to our own minds, our fears, our bitterness and our disdain for ourselves and others. In that state of diminished humanity and character we were incredibly dangerous. Most of us didn't intend to cause harm to anybody. We just did. We justified everything. We thought cruelty and dishonesty were the only way to survive. We were programmed in our addictions to create emotional, physical, financial, sexual harm in every direction—like whirlwinds of negativity and pain.

The harms we caused endure for a long time, sometimes for a lifetime. They can't be undone, unlike "hurts" which can be resolved with a simple, honest apology. We have to find ways to learn to live with them.

In contrast, hurts are just a part of life. Conflict comes with being human. Left to our own devices, hurts and harms often look and feel the same, so before we start trying to deal with the harms we have done, we need to find someone with good judgment to help us see which is which. For example, we don't get to hold ourselves forever accountable for schoolyard pranks (unless they turned into bullying), social clumsiness and every mistake of judgment we have ever made. We are not responsible for all the hurt in the world. What a relief.

Ironically, one common way of harming people is by trying so hard not to hurt their feelings that we never speak up for ourselves and never let ourselves be seen. We are actually being dishonest with them and depriving them of knowing who we are. These are the kinds of stealth harms that those around us—friends, families, co-workers and romantic partners—have no way of protecting themselves against. Our dishonesty will eventually reveal itself to us and to them, but usually very, very slowly.

Even at the level of dreams those of us with addictions are much better at picking up on the harms done to us than the ones we do, at least in the heat of the moment. Shockingly, our need for self-justification runs so deep that it can take years for us to let ourselves recognize the full scope of the damage we have done. The best clue that we are dealing with the ways we have harmed others is that an issue remains stubbornly unresolved in our dreams, sometimes for years. Eventually we allow the part we played in destructive situations to emerge, and slowly, over time we get the opportunity to take ownership for some of the darkest actions of our past.

Robert worked for too many years at a toxic, hierarchical institution where, in spite of his achievements, he was always treated as an outsider, as second class. He had long since lost heart but didn't have the courage to quit and go elsewhere. Eventually he and his employer parted on awkward, inconclusive terms, but in his dreams he kept returning there night after night, year after year. He could not shake the impression that he still had unfinished business with the place, but what?

Here is a dream he had ten years after leaving.

> *As Robert walks through the offices he finds that they have taken on a new, distorted shape. All the corridors have been blown open so he can see into the offices and find out what is in them. His is filled with exercise equipment and sofas. Those of his colleagues are filled with booze and weight machines. There is what looks like a dinosaur in the CEO's corner office.*

The administration is about to make an announcement about the future. Somehow the whole city is involved in the outcome. The office is to be downgraded and he is offered a chance to be sent to headquarters in a new city full of soaring spaces and established landmarks.

A troublesome long-time woman employee, with whom he often clashes, is unimpressed. Jaded as she is, she tells him nothing will happen for a long time. He goes out for a lunchtime walk.

He notices that, just outside her office, which is filled with beds, there is a black mink coat lying on the floor just like the one his mother had, but as he looks at it this one turns grey. On his way out he grabs a bottle of liquor from the office party that is going on.

What harm had Robert done in this crazy place that was full of beds and personal exercise equipment and booze? He seemed to fit right in and, although he was constantly demeaned there, he was still tempted to follow the corporate culture to another city. He had become part of it.

The revelation of the dream was that nobody actually did any work. They exercised, they sat on sofas or rested on beds, they drank, but, aside for awaiting pronouncements from on high, nobody did anything and nothing was really expected of them. He was still rehashing old resentments about his mother's lack of warmth, but that was about all he was doing.

He called the dream "Seeing the Distortion." His addictions had addled his sense of self and had left him in a funk of self-pity, paralysis and resentment. In such a barely-functioning, addiction-riddled company, where everybody acted the same way, he couldn't see what harm he had done. What was wrong with sitting around and schmoozing and taking money for it? The only harm he could see was that he had gotten stuck, but deep down he knew that every time he perpetuated the lack of values that went with his addiction he was actually doing harm, even if nobody around him could see it. It was quieter, deeper and more vicious than he had ever suspected. He realized that he was subtracting from life, always taking and giving nothing. This distortion of character had worked too well for him for too long. It was a way of dealing with the world that had to stop with him.

There was probably nothing Robert could do in such an unhealthy company to make amends, but he could, and did, change his work ethic and, like the drug addict avoiding the dealer, became acutely aware of staying out of slippery work environments.

The harms done in Joyce's dream are much more overtly dangerous than those in Robert's.

> *Joyce is driving a big, old red-colored Chevrolet in a muddy field. (Is it the same as her mother's? Maybe. She is not sure.) She is supposed to go to a meeting somewhere around here, but it is taking her a long time to find it. She is also supposed to be back at work already.*

She decides she has three major problems.

First, people have been shouting at her about the lights on her car but she has ignored them. She thinks her high beams work, but not her low beams. She is upset because this could be dangerous.

Second, she comes to a building, but when she puts on the brakes, they don't work. She goes right through a wall, demolishing a window in the process. She is scared because she already knew the brakes weren't working. It would be terrible if she knocked down the whole building, so she stops.

Third, she suddenly can't remember the third problem, but she knows she will have to call a repair person.

There is no time left to get to the meeting so she will have to get back to work. She is just starting a new job and doesn't know exactly where or when she is supposed to show up. 2:00 or 2:30 maybe? She will have to call them and tell them that she won't be coming back, ever. This is very anxiety-producing for her.

Joyce is all of us—in a frenzied swirl, creating havoc all around us and unable to see how dangerous we are to ourselves and others. We are at our most harmful when we are thinking of everything but what is right in front of us. But the harms are real and eventually we wake up to what we have done.

Everyone causes harm to someone else at some point, but our harms carry the special stamp of addiction— indifference to all suffering but our own.

Joyce was still living a version of her mother's life, perpetuating her mannerisms and mistakes and, like her, only indirectly conscious of her own impact on the world. (She called the dream, "Mom's Red Chevrolet.") But she couldn't put the blame on anyone else. Was Joyce responsible for the damage she was doing? Yes, absolutely. Harm is harm. There are no excuses. As far as the world is concerned we are our actions, actions that usually harm the people we are closest to the most.

Shelley thought of herself as a caring, but stressed and over-taxed, mother. She did her best.

> *Shelley is sitting on a dock holding onto a wooden piling while she watches a young boy, 4 or 5 years old, in a boat. He seems familiar, like her own son when he was little. The child's father, (her ex-husband), is doing something on the water at a distance from him.*
>
> *She holds on to the post and waits, but she becomes nervous and concerned. The father is taking too long and is unaware the tide is rising. The waves swamp the boy's boat but he does as he has been told and raises his hand to show that, although he has been using a breathing apparatus as he has been told to do, he is out of air. She is furious that the boy's father is being so neglectful. She wants to protect the boy but, although the father is signaling her to swim out, she doesn't think she can get to the child either, so she stays where she is.*
>
> *The whole scene is being narrated like a documentary.*
>
> *All of a sudden she is with the boy, holding him and trying to lift him up. They are both going under but she is not panicking. Others are nearby but they*

*can't reach them. She can't believe the father doesn't
realize how much trouble they are in.*

*She grabs the child and swims to the shore. The
waters become calm and the narrator announces that
the child is dead. He cannot be revived.*

*The dream ends with her feeling useless and
desperately sad. She is struck that the boy died
because he was so helpless. She thinks how much she
loved him, and how brave and trusting he was.*

*All she can do is make the empty gesture of
rubbing his back again and again.*

In the dream Shelley never does take action to save her
child. She observes and criticizes her former husband,
expecting him or others to be the rescuer. Somehow she is
magically transported to be with the boy when he dies and
quickly takes on the role of the grieving mother, focusing on
how vulnerable and good he was, and how much she loved
him.

This is the story being narrated in her brain, and she
makes herself both the victim and the heroine.

In her real life, her actual son did not die, but she could
never figure out why he who was so charming and outgoing
in the world was so distant and guarded with her. The dream,
which she called "The Drowning Child," confronted her
with how much she had wounded him with her passivity and
neglect, with her pernicious life-defying and self-serving
blandness. If she ever hoped to have a real relationship with
him she would have to make a conscious effort to take
ownership of what she had done and somehow make it up
to him in the time they still had ahead of them.

The range of harms for which we end up owing amends
is staggering and covers the full extent of human behavior.

From killing individuals or families by driving while drunk or high, to destroying reputations and destroying trust, to robbing children of their innocence, to knowingly infecting people with disease, to stealing people's life savings, to breaking the hearts of anyone kind enough to care about us. The list goes on and on. Whatever the harm we have caused, the principle is the same. There is only one meaningful way to atone for what we have done. We need to take responsibility for our actions and commit ourselves to doing everything humanly possible to repair the damage.

On some level we all realize that eventually we will have to own up to and make amends for all the harmful things we have done in the past. We know in the depths of our being that, unreleased, the weight of them will take us down.

Amends are scary, but having taken the first Seven Steps we have learned that we are people of character. We know that with the help of a Higher Power we will be able to find the strength to step up and tackle each harmful action, one by one, until they can all be safely relegated to the past where they belong.

STEP NINE

"Made direct amends to such people wherever possible, except when to do so would injure them or others."

The first moment we look directly into another person's eyes and admit we have harmed them and offer to do everything we possibly can to rectify the situation, we encounter our humanity at a whole new level. We ask for guidance, take a very deep breath and make our amends. We do not ask for forgiveness because we are meeting as equals and neither of us has the power to condemn or absolve the other, or to erase the past. We are both vulnerable. We are both coming face to face with the human condition—the very thing we as addicts have been trying to run away from for all these years.

For most of us this is the first time we actually pay full attention to another human being. We realize, with a shock, that they are just as real as we are, with their own set of perceptions and needs and reactions just as complete and all-consuming as our own. For most of us this comes as a revelation. In this moment we start to grow up.

They can accept or reject our overtures. How much tolerance and love they are capable of is on them. But we have taken our work in recovery out into the world. We are imperfect because everyone is imperfect. The only remedy we can offer for the injuries we have caused is our willingness to grow.

We are not terrible people. We may have done some terrible things to ourselves and others, but that does not define who we are. We are still human beings, infused with light.

The key is not to try to heal ourselves at the expense of others, to inflict more pain. Some of these people may have died, some may never want to see us again, but amends are still possible. We can treat "such" people, people like them, in such a way that, without anybody even knowing what we are doing, we are consciously changing our relationship to the people we harmed. A kindness to a stranger in trouble, a nod to an elderly person who reminds us of parents long dead, a smile, rather than a rebuke, to a child in distress, every supportive interaction with another person trying to recover—these have the power to shift everything in us and in our world.

So what do our dreams have to say about how our amends look from the inside?

Robert had yet another dream, six years after the one recounted in the last chapter and once again at the company where he worked many years before.

> *Robert is with another employee in the corner office of a CEO who is new to the job. They are working on some sort of plan to fix the company but fundamentally the place is a mess.*
>
> *They open the door for the new boss who brings with him an African-American client who he thinks he can use as leverage to make his employees, all of whom are white males, hide their grievances and be on their best behavior. Robert is busy clearing up a cot he has been lying on in a sort of sexual reverie, the place where he had been "caught" for many years.*

(Dreams are full of sneaky little puns and plays on words.)

The CEO viciously attacks his co-worker and fires him, though Robert survives. He quickly gets the measure of the man—dyed red hair and stained lower teeth that he exposes when he talks. Robert is aware that he has no strength of character. He looks like a weasel.

As Robert moves the cot away, the place becomes a gym with some excellent equipment. There are several healthy men exercising there who look up when he stumbles briefly on one of the machines.

Robert has been consciously changing his whole approach to work for 16 years by now, but amends can take a long time.

In the dream he is actually working and he even has a co-worker and is no longer totally isolated, though the fellow doesn't last long in this environment. The big change is that Robert clearly recognizes what a mess the place really is and he is no longer working for some vague authority figure in the corner office who only exists in his mind. He now sees who he is working for, a real person, someone who keeps people in line through vicious social manipulation and who really is nasty and feral. This knowledge gives Robert the chance to stop being a victim of his own fears and to take care of himself.

He stubs his toe (literally) on one of the pieces of equipment he needs to get healthy, but he is now surrounded by other people doing their own work, people who are quietly looking out for him. He called the dream, "No More Cot."

Some people ask if we should put ourselves at the top of the list of those we have harmed. We can if we want, but we don't really need to. We *are* the list. It is all about us. Every harsh, cruel thing we have ever done to others we have actually done to ourselves. We have known this all along. We have been secretly punishing and martyring ourselves by hiding behind our addictions for long enough. We have treated ourselves worse than anyone but another addict could ever imagine. Now the greatest amends we can make to ourselves is to step up, own what we have done and set ourselves free.

Each individual amends we make eventually turns into something bigger. Over time we start to discover that we have begun to live our lives differently.

Tom was in the process of making a series of formal amends when he had the following dream:

> *Tom's father has just published a long, soppy article in* The New York Times *about Tom's death (even though he is clearly not dead yet). He expresses, in operatic terms, that the death of his only son means that he can never have grandchildren. This to him would be the ultimate tragedy.*
>
> *Tom is particularly furious because, as usual, his father manages to appropriate all pain and all feeling for himself.*
>
> *Tom is then sitting in a meeting opposite a woman who is dark and pretty and who is trying to convey that she understands loss, but there is a man sitting between them.*

How dare Tom be so public facing his fears and stepping up to take ownership of who he is and what he has done? He is contradicting everything he was ever taught by his father—that the truth doesn't matter, that life is all about self-interest. All these amends Tom is making are a threat to the old order and the behaviors of generations before him. The old regime dies hard. Its reign of self-pity and self-absorption doesn't end without a fight, the more outrageous the better—right in the pages of *The New York Times*.

He is literally going against his entire history but, as the dream suggests, the compensations happen fast. A young woman who understands what he is going through appears. She is not immediately available, but she is only one person away and she is making an effort to connect with him. Who knows what possibilities could open for the two of them to build a different kind of life together? Tom called the dream, "Not Dead Yet."

When we finally make our amends everything changes, and the list traditionally known as the Ninth Step "Promises" of Alcoholics Anonymous starts to come true. The very things we thought we would get from pursuing our addictions—freedom, happiness, acceptance of the past, confidence that we will be taken care of, ease with the people around us, real connections, an open heart, a sense of value, release from anxiety and fear, even pleasure and delight—all these start to happen, and more, but this time they are not just seductive fantasies, the illusion of a rich, passionate life fueled by our addictions. Now they are real, even better, richer, deeper than we could have expected, because we have taken steps to become real people in the real world. These promises may be elusive but we have earned them, and we can trust that they will be available when we need them.

Sadly our amends around the big issues in our lives don't necessarily trickle down to annoying encounters in the subway or on the highway, or stubborn arguments that flare up out of nowhere with the people we love. We quickly resort to being stubborn and certain we are right. All of a sudden we are at a loss, defending our own childishness, and helpless to break through to a more adult way of behaving.

Carla had a dream about just such a conflict, which she called "Betrayal."

> *Carla and her boyfriend, Andrew, are at a country fair. She goes off by herself to buy him a blueberry muffin, something he has never tried before. He waits for her at the bar and she thinks how great it is that she can trust him with other women who might be there.*
>
> *She is talking with a friend, Dan, when she sees his eyes widen at something that is going on behind her. When she turns around she sees her boyfriend and another woman making out.*
>
> *She walks right up to him and confronts him. He is shocked and just stands there. She says she can't believe it. She trusted him and never thought that he would betray her. She demands that he explain himself but as she continues to yell and give voice to her pain and grief and disappointment, he gets into a white van, (not the fancy sports car he has in real life), and drives away.*
>
> *She drops to her knees and wails out a series of declarations. This will change the course of her life forever. Nothing will ever be the same again. She will never trust anyone again, ever, ever. Of all people, how could he do this to her?*
>
> *She cries and cries and then begins to doubt what she has seen. Maybe his little dalliance didn't really mean anything to Andrew and she should*

overlook it. Then she finds herself in her mother's backyard, full of dead leaves. She too had been cheated on many times.

Her friend Dan tries to console her by offering her a plate of crumbs.

None of this had actually happened. It was all about her fear, as embodied in the dream by Dan. She hadn't even seen Andrew cheating until she saw it through his eyes. But when she woke up she was still profoundly upset, convinced it was real. She never wanted to see Andrew again. Three thoughts kept running through her head. First, she had always vowed that if anyone cheated on her she would have to leave. (She would not make the same mistakes her mother had.) Second, she couldn't believe how much Andrew had loved her. She remembered that when she was with him she felt as if she would never feel unloved again. Third, he had been perfect for her. She would never find anyone like him again.

Poor Andrew. What pressure. He didn't have a chance. She had rules and expectations for relationships in general and particularly for him that he knew nothing about. Neither of them knew it, but she was setting him up to fail. As a final indignity, she even sent him off in a bland white van, denying him the option of driving his own car.

The operatic intensity and the sweeping declarations of her reaction were the clue that something dangerous was going on. She was having a full-fledged tantrum and she was intent on destroying the relationship.

We can often do much more harm with our minds than we do with our actions. Our victims have no idea what has happened to them. We change and move on, and they have no idea what hit them. It is the thoughts behind our actions that create all the chaos, and it is at this level that we have to be ready to amend our behaviors or we will continue to revert to type and do the same harmful things again and again.

What good does it do to amend our outward behavior and repair our relationships with our loved ones if we are still determined to mistrust them and browbeat them into following our rules? How have we changed? What is the point of returning money that we owe, only to secretly keep angling for special treatment in our business dealings? What does it mean to have years of recovery and still get tripped up by exactly the same petty annoyances that have always set us off? Of course we all have the right to be as imperfect as we want to be, but how deep do our amends actually go?

One of the unintended consequences of starting to act like an adult, even if only briefly, is that we begin to notice when we are acting like children. It takes us a while to learn how to be the person we are and, at the same time, to accept the rich, mysterious and often frustrating humanness of others.

No one likes making amends. Most of us will do anything we can to avoid them, and in this way the Ninth Step becomes a kind of external conscience for many of us. We do the right thing because we do not want to have to clean up the mess we are about to get ourselves into. We will eventually need to find deeper, more personal reasons than that to behave well. We continue to find out in the Steps ahead how to live a more expansive, genuinely grown-up life than we could ever have imagined.

STEP TEN

"Continued to take personal inventory and when we were wrong promptly admitted it."

Stay awake, stay conscious and don't quit. The single most dangerous thing those of us in recovery can do is declare victory and coast. We have seen it happen again and again. We lighten up on meetings, fall out of touch with our program support network, forget everything we have learned, and the next thing we know we are counting days after a slip—if we are lucky. Some of us end up dead. This can happen after years and years of recovery, always a shock, always deeply disturbing, and always, in hindsight, predictable.

Consistent choices and addiction don't mix.

So we don't stop. We have cleaned up the past and now we turn to the ongoing task of cleaning up the present. We must act promptly. Up to this point we have had to take as long as necessary on each Step. Now we start to confront the issue of time. We begin to realize that all the years stunted by our addictions can never be reclaimed. We wake up to the fact that the time we have is finite and we can no longer afford to waste any of it.

Of course we continue to get on the wrong track and make mistakes, but now the goal is to learn from them and take action to correct them as soon as we make them. We are building character in the real world.

We also get a chance to observe and learn from the experiences of others and, as we ourselves wake up, we come to appreciate how important the factor of time is for all of us in our healing. We hear about plateaus and breakthroughs— the terrible self-assurance of year two, the five-year doldrums, the new energy after seven years, the slog around year ten, the unfamiliar sense of relaxation after fifteen years, the huge shift in perception around the mid-twenties, and the new, highly personal depth and sense of strength that come with more than thirty years. The pattern is different for everyone but we begin to pick up on a quiet folk wisdom about what we can expect.

By staying close to the program and paying attention, we gather evidence that the Steps work at every stage of life. They are able to offer comfort and guidance whatever we might be facing—the challenges of youth, of extreme old age, or of everything in between.

Dan and Carl had grown up together and eventually they opened a real estate office in the little town where they were born. Both had to face addiction in themselves and in those around them. They both took silent pride in the fact that by getting into recovery together they had saved each other's lives. Eventually they did well together and prospered. They even invested together in some commercial properties in the region. Their children played together on local sports teams and their families were considered pillars of the community. Then Dan had a disturbing dream.

> *It is late at night and Carl is still in the office. Dan, seeing the lights still on, comes by to make sure he is OK. When Dan comes in, Carl is startled and*

*furtively slips the papers he is working on under
another folder. They do their usual banter about both
being so obsessive about work and Dan leaves, telling
his partner he shouldn't work so hard.*

The dream left Dan troubled and he couldn't seem to let
it go. He was sure that he and Carl had no secrets from each
other, and yet in the dream Carl was clearly up to something
sneaky.

As Dan discussed the dream he came to the conclusion
that, because he trusted his friend so completely, it was a sign
that he himself needed to be more straightforward in his own
business dealings. He had been willing to cut a few corners
recently and he felt that something was telling him to clean
up his act.

For the next few months Dan followed his intuition and
was very scrupulous about everything he did. One beautiful
autumn morning a pair of government auditors appeared at
their office armed with a warrant and began a thorough
examination of their books. The news was not good. Carl
had gotten himself into some very complicated and shady
business transactions that eventually landed him in jail. Dan
was devastated, but because his record was so transparent he
was cleared of any involvement. Eventually he was able to
weather the fallout and the scandal with his reputation intact.

Dan hadn't changed his behavior because of any outside
pressure, but because something in him, an intuition, told
him it was the right thing to do. The dream, which he called
"Keeping It Clean," shows the mechanics of developing a
conscience. Dan acted, not on some predetermined set of
external values, but rather based on his experiences of getting
things wrong in the past, on the mistakes he had made that
came to light as he took an ongoing inventory of himself. He

chose to learn from them and act in real time in ways that would make him comfortable in his own skin.

This is hard, unrelenting work, but the payoff is a life where we know we can tap into a guidance system on how to act in any situation. Continuous self-awareness is the key.

One of the mistakes we begin to notice at this stage of our recovery is that many of us have conflated or confused our addictions with other underlying issues that often drove us into our addictive behaviors in the first place. As we continue to examine the reasons we act the way we do, we can begin to separate out a whole set of other issues.

> *Catherine is sitting in a lovely, tepid wading pool contentedly playing with a baby. She is talking amiably with her therapist who is standing, dressed in his usual suit and tie and loafers, right at the edge of the water.*
>
> *Just below the surface she catches a glimpse of a bright green rat with glowing red eyes. She warns her therapist that something is wrong, but just as he tells her not to worry, the rat instantaneously grabs the baby and disappears with it down a drain, leaving only a piece of skin tissue floating nearby.*

Catherine was horrified. She had no trouble naming the dream. It was "The Green Rat." She had been in recovery and in therapy for many years when she had this dream and had recently been considering stopping therapy altogether because she was doing so well. The dream felt like a serious and ugly setback.

It was certainly graphic and it definitely grabbed her attention. But what was the message? What was threatening the burgeoning new life she was experiencing? What was lurking below the surface that threatened her recovery? She decided to take the dream seriously and the next time she had an appointment with her therapist she let him know that he needed to stop being complacent and reassuring her that everything was fine. She insisted that they work together to find out the nature of the deadly threat still hiding from view. She was committed to her personal inventory and she was determined to make sure that the professional help she got was just as invested in finding the truth as she was.

Fortunately her therapist got the message that they had been missing something very important and started to refocus. Initially he and Catherine looked at the vicious part of herself that always killed off love almost before it began, the cruel intensity with which she killed off hope, the way she glamorized despair. Over time, with her therapist's help, Catherine was able to face a deeply buried history of physical and sexual abuse during her childhood. As long as it remained hidden it was a threat to her recovery, so it came as a great relief for her to get the chance to separate out her addiction from her personal wounds. She could be confident that her recovery would be resilient, no matter what other issues came up.

Many of us have our own versions of the glittering green rat, the spoiler that seems to strike us out of nowhere. We are not just addicts. We often struggle with depression, (as did Bill Wilson who came up with the Steps in the first place), with various other mental health issues, with histories of abuse and trauma, with physical illness and a host of other conditions as well. It is tempting to focus solely on our Twelve Step recovery and ignore everything else, but it is simply too dangerous. The taste for freedom that we get from treating our addictions gives us the courage to keep going, to do everything we can to clean out all the other mental and emotional stumbling blocks that hold us back. In recovery we develop a passionate desire for health in every part of our life.

William had been in recovery for several decades and, because he was still feeling stuck and resentful of his parents, both long dead, he decided to write each of them a letter in order to articulate just how angry he still was with both of them. He had never been able to shake it no matter what he did. He had prayed for them, tried to find forgiveness in his heart for them, spent endless therapy sessions talking about them, but he knew he was stuck in a resentment which he began to fear might never be lifted. What was he doing wrong?

He was extremely embarrassed to put into words the intensity and primitiveness of his feelings, but he persevered. A few days after he wrote to his mother he was shocked and horrified to have this dream.

> *William is in his parents' house. He is about twelve or thirteen years old. His mother, as she often does, raises a coat hanger to hit him with. He starts to fight and grabs her by her feet and swings her around. She becomes elastic as if she has no bones, like taffy. She writhes and twists and manages to fight back at him. He is afraid she is going to kill him. There is a long table in the kitchen and, still holding on to her feet, he slams her whole body down on it. His mind goes into overdrive. He knows he has killed her. He is certain that she is not just unconscious, but he thinks that this is not murder either. He stares in disbelief down at the table, but she is no longer there.*

William was shaken to his core by this dream. After all his dedicated work on himself, this was not the kind of person he thought he had become, certainly not the person he wanted to be. He labeled it starkly, "Murdering My Mother."

He was even more confused to realize that, in the days following the dream, he began experiencing a lightness of spirit that he had never felt before. He was full of energy and good feeling, an unfamiliar buoyancy. How could this be happening?

The thought began to form in his mind that he had spent his whole life protecting his mother, refusing to hold her accountable, at great cost to himself. In the dream he finally allowed himself to experience the extent of his own anger. Judging it, holding it down all these years, had taken a huge amount of energy. He thought he had a resentment (a stuck feeling), but he had never allowed himself to feel the horror of what he had experienced as a child in the first place.

With the deftness and precision to be found in dreams, William's mother quickly becomes an effigy of herself—not quite real, but a kind of shape-shifting comic-book villain. In that state William is able to grab her by the feet (the place where she stands within him) and with one sweeping gesture knock the life out of her. Suddenly she and any power she might still have over him disappear. When he wakes up he is still so concerned about his mother that he can't see that by killing this monster in his mind he is acting in self-defense. He is actually fighting for his life.

And no one in the real world gets hurt. Continuing to explore as William did is not for the faint of heart or for the beginner, but not confronting the past is a kind of lie we tell ourselves. We can't afford that and eventually we have to start telling ourselves the truth.

William was at last ready to be released from the mistaken but deeply-held idea that it was his duty to protect his mother's memory at all costs. He had planned to go to his grave without allowing himself to feel the pain and rage he wasn't allowed to have as a child. As a result he ended up stifling all his feelings including the positive ones.

We all know the loss that we experienced when we stopped growing internally as our addictions took us over. We know the terrible sadness of putting on a brave face like good little boys and girls and fundamentally refusing to change. We have a lot of time to make up for. None of us can afford to get stuck like this ever again.

Fortunately the Steps and the support of the fellowship give us a way to walk through pain so we are not overwhelmed. We learn that we are not victims of the darkness we have encountered in the world and in ourselves. We no longer need to destroy ourselves in a desperate attempt to escape it.

Our greatest weapon is surrender. The decision we made back in Step Three to turn over our will and our lives to a power greater than ourselves is based on the premise that the more we surrender the more we will be cared for. So day after day we move forward, butting up against reality in ways large and small, making mistakes, telling the truth about them, learning to recognize when we are going the wrong direction, and slowly discovering that we have become a person of conscience. Although we could never have imagined such a thing happening before recovery, we find out that living with integrity feels quite natural, as if this is who we were meant to be all along.

STEP ELEVEN

"Sought through prayer and meditation to improve our consapple contact with God as we understood Him, praying only for knowledge of His will for us and the power to carry that out."

Ever since we humans started to contemplate the possibility that there was some sort of higher order shaping our reality we have turned to forms of prayer and meditation to try to open our minds to larger realms. We are all seekers.

Each of us is like a goldfish swimming around in a bowl seeing only our own reflection and trying to contemplate the nature of water. We see only the shadow of the hand that sprinkles fish food on the surface at regular intervals when we get hungry. We have no way to conceive of what kind of being is taking care of us or why we are being fed. We cannot possibly picture the grocery store where these delicious flakes come from, or the elaborate international delivery system that brought this little box of food from a manufacturer on the other side of a world that is totally beyond our capacity to imagine.

We can either take the suggestion to pray and mediate as a directive and double down on one form of practice or another, or we can take it as a generous, warm invitation to open ourselves to the whole history of mankind's search for something larger. We can embrace all of it and find out what parts of it work for each of us, perhaps finding or rediscovering a religious tradition that fits us perfectly, or possibly assembling a personal combination of beliefs and practices that is uniquely our own.

The Twelve Steps came out of a specific time and place and culture, a United States emerging from years of crippling economic depression, social unrest and rumors of war. The founders were very practical people, white, middle-aged, middle- and upper-class males, mostly Christian, trying to find their place in the driven, highly materialistic societies of New York and Akron, Ohio. No surprise that the God of their understanding was a "Him" and looked like they did. Though many of them had rejected the Christianity of their childhood, some were drawn to religious-based moral revival movements such as the Oxford Group. Still, the idea of using intense introspective prayer and meditation practices in search of more direct conscious contact with the divine would have seemed very foreign to them, well outside their frame of reference. Most likely they would have initially been taken aback, considering such behaviors, even though they could very well save their lives, to be unmanly, weak and frivolous.

From our current vantage point, when we have all become world citizens and amateur psychologists, it is easy to overlook just how radical and open-minded such ideas were for their time. This Step opens with an invitation to learn, to explore the realm of consciousness itself, to stop long enough to allow ourselves to be thrilled that it exists in us at all. Like life itself, consciousness is at once something so extraordinary that nobody has been able to explain it and yet so common that we all take it for granted. Here we are invited to expand our own direct experience of connecting with whatever it is that animates our lives, building on all the wisdom on the subject that humankind has accumulated up to now. This connection is probably more readily available than we think—in ideas that float to the surface when we are silent and receptive, or in new perspectives that come when we meditate on a dream.

> *Lars is standing in the middle of a river in the region of Scandinavia where he grew up. He is struck by how remote the place is. There are none of the usual summer cottages around. The water is cold, murky and brownish-yellow in color. He is up to his armpits. Although he cannot see the bottom he can feel sharp stones under his feet. The water is flowing quite fast and it takes all his effort to keep himself upright. Lars is there because he is trying to get to the source of the river, far upstream, but he is frustrated. The more time and energy he spends pressing forward, the farther he feels he is from reaching his goal.*
>
> *Instantly he is now standing in the same river up to his knees but further downstream. Here the water is flowing more slowly, but it is clear and warm. He is standing on sand, which he can see through the light reflecting off the smooth surface. He takes in the scene. It is beautiful. He didn't get to the source but he decides that what he sees here is much better.*

This is the same river. Who Lars is and where he chooses to stand make all the difference. Is he there to conquer the river, to chart its course, to measure its length? Or is he there to experience the river? Why do we recover? To master life? Or to live it? In the dream, which he called, "The Source Is Right Here," Lars got an answer spontaneously from deep within himself. He began to appreciate the beauty to be had by putting down his endless striving. That turns out to be just another form of being in charge, of not being here, which we mistake in our addict's mind as a way of keeping ourselves safe. Have we ever actually stopped long enough to breathe, let alone meditate or pray? Do we dare let ourselves be more fully conscious?

Perhaps by this stage in our recovery we have been rendered humble and authentic enough to realize that reality as we experience it is all we will ever know of God, so we had better start paying attention to life in a whole new way. Up to now we have likely held on to the last traces of our precious defiance and resistance, but now is the time to own up to any deep-seated, global resentments we still have about being human, and start aligning ourselves with the flow of life and placing ourselves squarely in the middle of it.

Ironically, we who came into recovery powerless and broken now need knowledge and power more than ever, but knowledge and power beyond our own. Alignment is the key.

When Regina's sponsor of over twenty years died after a brief illness, Regina felt as if she had died too. It was as if she had lost everyone she had ever loved all at once. She didn't know how she could go on.

> *Regina's sponsor is standing at a blackboard with an old-fashioned pointer in her hand. The board is filled with the words of the Serenity Prayer written out again and again. Looking intently at Regina she methodically goes from prayer to prayer as if willing her to concentrate on every word in each one.*
>
> *"God grant me the Serenity to accept the things I cannot change, the Courage to change the things I can, and the Wisdom to know the difference."*

As she points out the words she offers quiet
reassurances, like a murmured chant, that everything
will be all right, that Regina will be taken care of.

Regina's grief and her sense of loss and disorientation
were slow to pass, but after the dream, which she titled
simply, "The Serenity Prayer," she found a new sense of
certainty in herself that, whatever happened, she would be in
good hands. She also discovered a new urgency and focus in
her prayers.

Death is the essential reality in our lives that we cannot
change. Like it or not, our Higher Power's will for each of us
is that we and the people we love are going to die. Why this
is so remains a deeply confounding mystery, but the mere
fact that we know death is coming makes our search for
meaning and engagement with a God of our understanding
that much more intense. How can we confront reality
without resorting to the old distractions of our fears and our
addictions? Do we have the strength and courage to take
action, to be engaged in life in the face of the inevitable?

The serenity Prayer is about learning to live in and co-
operate with reality. The Eleventh Step is about learning to
live in and co-operate with a Higher Power. Perhaps the two
are the same. We start by accepting reality, allowing ourselves
to be guided as to what our part in it is, and then summoning
up the confidence from a source beyond us to step up and
do what we are called upon to do.

Ultimately Regina's "only" task in the face of her great
loss is to find a conscious inner connection with a source of
knowledge and power she can trust. Nothing else matters.

Virtually all of us have had the experience, however brief
and however long ago, of finding ourselves in alignment with
life. Maybe just for an instant we heard a song, felt a human

touch, saw something so beautiful we could hardly stand it, and we were at home with the world around us. This is the place where our prayer and meditation can lead us. This is the ground on which we can build a lovingly restored life.

Jessica came into recovery at a very young age and after many years of program she had this dream.

> *Jessica is at the theater watching a wonderful actress she admires perform in a play with many less talented actors. Jessica realizes that while the others make the actress look good, she as a member of the audience becomes increasingly uncomfortable.*
>
> *She recognizes and identifies with the actress's dilemma. Jessica can see how much such a great talent needs to be around other exceptional actors if she really wants to make her performance extraordinary.*

Why would such a talented actress limit herself by not working with people who would challenge her to stretch her abilities? If any of us want to know what God's will is for us, it is clearly for us to develop our God-given talents to the full. We are not born to be less than the best version of ourselves.

Thinking about the dream, Jessica wondered if in her long-term recovery she had become complacent with the benefits she experienced and had ceased to challenge herself. Was she being as open and vulnerable and ready to grow as she had been? She knew from experience that every time she had taken the risk to expand her horizons she had found the inner strength she needed.

Jessica called the dream, "The Leading Lady." She had given up the role of producer, director and stage manager of her life, but what did it mean, long term, to be the central character in her own life? How well was she doing?

The Eleventh Step gives us a chance to step back and look at the larger picture of our recovery, a chance to reflect. Imagine how the Steps would work if this one were removed. We would still have a practical and probably effective blueprint on how to recover from our addictions, but we would always be caught up with all the drama they stir up. They would never be put into perspective and we would never realize how much bigger each of us is than they are.

Consciousness, and with it the ability to look at our actions, is what makes alignment and acceptance possible. Without it we would never know when we were out of kilter and at odds with the world. It is also what makes us want to seek for meaning and strive for clarity. Without it Jessica could never conceive of the drive for quality that would make an actress like the one in her dream want to improve simply because she could.

One unorthodox and rather cheeky way to look at the story of Adam and Eve is that when they were at one with life they experienced paradise, but when they gave in to their pettiness and small-mindedness (in modern terms, the reptilian part of the brain that sees only predator or prey) they started to judge themselves and the world around them as good or evil, separating themselves from the natural order of things. They weren't expelled from a state of purity and innocence. They ended up punishing and exiling themselves. That is what our addictions did to us. The Eleventh Step is a reminder that, whatever we have been though, somewhere in each of us we can find a place of wholeness that we can start to rely on in our daily lives.

This is also a chance to pause and take in how far we have come and how fundamentally changed we have been by the previous Steps. Prayer and meditation offer us the long slow embrace of life that we need. We are not the people we were when we first came into recovery. Like the other talented actors Jessica was looking for in the dream, we have been surrounded by people in recovery who have proven themselves exceptional, who have carried us and allowed us to develop beyond what we could ever have expected when we began.

Michael had a dream that captured all that change in one brief, resonant image.

> *Michael and someone else are going up the gangplank as they board a cruise ship. He catches a glimpse of his father standing behind him to the left. Without a pause he says over his shoulder, "Bye, dad," and walks on.*

The moment seems so innocuous and fleeting in the telling, but to Michael the dream was huge. He gave it the ironic name, "Thanks a Lot, Dad," suggesting that he wasn't quite as detached as he appeared and still held onto a twinge of resentment and maybe always would. Nonetheless for him the dream represented an almost unimaginable inner accomplishment, the work of over twenty-five years in recovery programs.

His estranged father was a raging, multi-addicted abuser and a brute who had attacked and demeaned him mercilessly all his life. Michael could do nothing right. He tried to find relief and oblivion in addictions to food, alcohol, and heartless perfectionism and self-blame. Nothing worked. The odds of Michael's ever escaping from the physical, mental and emotional tyranny in which he grew up were virtually zero. But he did.

Using the Steps as the core of his recovery that included every other form of healing he could find, over the years Michael slowly was able to find and befriend the essential part of himself that his father had done everything in his power to destroy. It was the greatest accomplishment of his existence and a victory beyond belief that Michael could walk calmly away from this man and get on with his life.

Throughout his recovery, no matter what Step he was on, Michael came to rely on prayer and meditation to reveal how to accept the reality of whatever situation he might be in, and to learn to focus on the next action to take that would be right for him. He found he had access to precisely the knowledge and power he needed, or as he phrased it, "I relaxed on the inside."

STEP TWELVE

"Having had a spiritual awakening as a result of these steps, we tried to carry this message to alcoholics, and to practice these principles in all our affairs."

So what is a spiritual awakening? Some lofty goal? A big payoff that will either strike us suddenly or that we will have to earn after a long, arduous apprenticeship?

The word "spiritual" is a dangerous one. Over the centuries the people most eager to use it to describe themselves have turned out to be neither kind nor tolerant of others. Like people who label themselves "beautiful," their lack of humility makes their judgment suspect.

Put simply, a "spiritual awakening" means that our spirits wake up. Nothing abstract or mystical about that. Our spirits do it every morning, if we let them.

We have all watched a newcomer arrive in the rooms, benighted, desperate and lost, and then, if they keep showing up, seen the change in their eyes, in their posture and in their whole demeanor. The lights come on.

Cause and effect. This is what happens when we apply the Twelve Steps to our lives. We were the ones always looking for the secret manual on how to live that everybody else seemed to have gotten but we never did. Now we have the tools and we want everybody to know what has happened to us. Not so easy.

We can "try" to carry this message, but we immediately bump up against reality. We are powerless over getting other people to change. We are right back at Step One. People still trapped in their addictions don't want to hear, and literally cannot hear, what we have to say. We were exactly the same before we started our recovery. And that is the saving grace. We have been exactly where they are. We are the only people who have any chance of getting through to them. We share the bond of suffering.

How do we pass on the principles we have put into place in our lives? By living them. And that has the power to change everything. When our spirits wake up there is no way we can *not* carry the message. We are the message and we can't help passing it on as long as we keep practicing what we have learned. In doing so, by carrying it to newcomers, by passing it back and forth among ourselves in a vast network of mutual education, we continually save each other's lives.

Joel had a vivid dream about his efforts to communicate his experience of waking up. This one stood out to him because it made him look at how fundamentally he and his outlook on life had changed. He called it "Teaching."

> *Joel is asked to chair a meeting and he starts talking about his experience of loss. He has lost almost everything in his life and very nearly his life itself, but most painful for him is the loss of his profession as a pediatric surgeon and along with it his prestige in other people's eyes, not to mention his substantial income. These were the only things that gave him meaning before recovery.*
>
> *In the dream Joel wrestles publicly with the ongoing conflict in his mind and tries to teach those*

in the meeting what he has learned. He tries to talk about hope but as an example he comes up with Sisyphus, the figure in classical mythology who is punished for his pride by being forced to roll a rock uphill for all eternity.

Sisyphus is usually seen as a symbol of hopelessness but in the dream Joel refuses to see him as a victim dully rolling a rock uphill only to have it roll down again. Rather, he tells his audience, he is a courageous being with "hope in his loins." Joel becomes more and more animated and passionate because clearly he is talking about himself. He points out to them that in all the repetitiveness, the pain, Sisyphus is still alive and that if he, Joel, had not learned in his recovery how to manage loss and find the value of hope without demands or conditions, he would never have survived to talk to them, let alone realize that such things as feelings or an inner life existed.

Joel was surprised at how forceful and engaged he became in the dream. Where had that come from? Before recovery he had been horrified by the drudgery, flatness and ordinariness of life. He thought he needed his addictions to make it interesting. They made it a nightmare.

Now he found himself talking about finding hope in existence itself, whether it was working out the way he wanted it to or not. Suffering and ordinariness were no longer intolerable and he could take comfort that each moment alive had a meaning of its own.

In many ways those of us in recovery are like the creatures found living near thermal vents at the bottom of the ocean. We shouldn't exist, but we do. And the only reasonable response is gratitude.

Who have we become? We have somehow turned into people of integrity, people who have principles. This is a long way from the days when, deep into protecting our addictions, we couldn't lower our standards fast enough to keep up with our behaviors.

And what exactly are the principles that we are trying to put into practice? Certainly honesty is key, along with kindness and tolerance for ourselves and others, but notably they are not spelled out in detail. They are not being imposed on us. Rather we get to define the principles of the program for ourselves as we go along and in the process they gradually become our own. Over time they prove themselves to be the basis of what makes for a good life.

We cannot practice them perfectly. We are just asked to "try" to practice them. It is a lifetime undertaking. We quickly find that having principles and applying them are two different things. One day a principled solution for a particular problem works, but the next day when we apply it to a similar situation, it falls flat. We are constantly forced to stay alert and keep refining our understanding of how our principles work.

To her program friends it seemed that Joan had been in recovery forever. She was a fixture in her regular meetings. She sponsored lots of people and always had wise and useful things to say. She had a series of health problems and was dealing with her advancing age with great humor and grace. This was her dream.

> *Joan is all dressed up and ready to go to a dance. She is very excited because, since she was a girl, dances have stood out as the most memorable and enjoyable*

events of her life. She is with friends and as they approach the hall they run into a series of barriers. There are several entrances but they are shut out at all of them.

At first she encounters a chain-link fence, then a locked door, a boarded-up window and a metal gate. She can hear the music inside and is determined to get in. There are lots of potential entrances, each with a light over it, so she goes back and forth, randomly trying them all.

Suddenly all the lights come on like at a carnival or on a television game show. The way opens and she is in a dance that is everything she has ever imagined.

She dances one dance and then finds herself outside, locked out again until she finds another combination of approaches that will get her back in. She repeats the process many times because the pure joy of being at the dance is worth all the effort.

Joan called the dream "The Right Sequence." Applying principles to all our affairs is not as simple or straightforward as we might hope. Direct action doesn't always work. Maybe we should try patience for a while. What are the limits of acceptance? When should we speak up? Every principle of the program seems to be balanced by its opposite.

Joan's health challenges tested her beliefs and principles in ways she had never anticipated. She knew from experience that her hard-won principles always worked, but in her new, almost daily, reality of doctors and diagnoses, she knew she had to use them with a new level of skill and discernment to be able to live the life she wanted while she still could.

We are all in the same situation. Every time we choose to apply a principle in our lives we need to call on every resource around us and within us to ask if the timing is right. It is said that not even the simplest musical scale can ever be played precisely the same way more than once. There are infinite variations of tone, pressure and speed in every repetition. So too, every moment of every day is like no other. The way we apply the principles we have learned must change constantly.

Sometimes we need to give our trust with abandon. Sometimes we need to step back and think things through. Sometimes we need to engage with life. Sometimes we need to surrender. Sometimes we need to find our voice. Sometimes we need to keep silent. Which principle fits right now? We get better at being the people of integrity that we want to be, but we have to keep practicing.

For those of us who were taught as children that "trying" was not enough and that we had to succeed or else, it comes as a relief to learn as adults that "trying" to carry the message or "trying" to practice our principles is all that can reasonably be expected of us in the first place, as the fallible, all-too-human beings that we are.

This way of life takes effort and courage. One long-term member at the end of his life was constantly being taken to the emergency room to deal with new and life-threatening complications. Whenever he was put in an ambulance or wheeled into an operating room he would remind everyone around him that all these professional people had trained for many years just so they could be there at that moment, ready to provide him with the finest care possible. His deeply held principle of gratitude never deserted him.

In all our affairs. When we ask what is the most important thing that has happened in our lives on any given day, the answer is usually not a big, obvious event but the tiny, infinitesimal moments that go almost unnoticed. These are what reveal the way we are really practicing the principles we have learned: our warm genuine interaction with the cashier at the supermarket checkout; a flash of awareness that a power greater than ourselves has taken care of some issue that has defied us; or something as fleeting as noticing the dazzle of autumn light on water.

We realize that in the earlier Steps we referred to "our life" as if it belonged to us. It does not. We slowly "get" that life owns us and our part is to live it and improve the lives of our fellow humans wherever we can. An added bonus is that, in doing so, we find out we are able to give much more than we receive. Most mysterious.

Alex was a big, gregarious man whose job was auctioning off lots of seafood at a commercial fish market. He was struck by the gentleness of this dream. (With a palpable sense of relief, they calm down the longer we stay in recovery.)

> *Alex is in a garden which is open to the public but no one else is there. He knows he is allowed in but he is slightly apprehensive about being there. He comes across a place where a power cord is plugged in. He follows it and walks beyond rows of neatly planted flowers and vegetables. He meets an ancient gardener and the two men chat like old friends.*
>
> *The old gentleman tells him how important it is to keep the cord safely above the plants so as not to damage them. He tells Alex that he will have to unplug the cord and find a new power source for it in the gardener's shed each time he wants to go further afield.*
>
> *As he walks through the garden he encounters a young woman in a pretty summery dress sitting alone on a bench. He recognizes that she too is in recovery.*

> *She tells him that her desire is to be able to "plan"*
> *the way other people do.*

Alex is struck by her loveliness. She seems very familiar to him and at first he thinks she might be his daughter or one of his granddaughters. He feels very protective of her. Who is she? And what is she trying to tell him?

Alex calls the dream, "The Power Cord." Why, he wonders, does he need a power cord in a garden, a place of natural growth and order? The answer is to trim, to mow, to till, to prune, to care for it without damaging the new growth. The work is constant and unending, just like his recovery. And just like recovery he always needs fresh new connections available that will allow him to stretch as far as he needs to. He needs to keep returning to the kindly but mysterious old gardener's cottage, connecting to a source of power greater than himself that will expand its reach as he does.

Alex is impressed that his dream literally presents the concept of a Higher Power in such practical, down-to-earth terms. These he can easily relate to, but where he gets confused is by the lovely, feminine young woman whose sole desire is the same as his. She asks only for basic predictability, the ability to put chaos behind her, to make plans, to be "normal," even serene. For this brusque, no-nonsense guy, it comes as a shock that she could be a part of him. The dream makes the introduction. It is up to them to develop a relationship.

Looking at the people who have relentlessly applied the principles of recovery for thirty, forty, fifty years, we get to witness them plugging constantly into new sources of power. As Alex is invited to do, they expand. The old protective shell of their addictions cracks open. They settle naturally into living in their own skins. Laughter breaks out, lightness of spirit, engagement, wonder, respect for the adventure, and awe at the immensity of it.

Gloriously individual and imperfect as they may be, they are living proof to the rest of us of just how much the Twelve Steps have to offer. They remind us that, beyond the pain, beyond the heartbreak, over the years in recovery each of us has been befriended by life, and on a daily basis, as long as we live, we each have the chance to gratefully befriend it back.

MORE THOUGHTS

Like our dreams, we addicts are always contending with oblivion, with not being here, escaping into nothingness. One drink, one high, one lapse in behavior and we are gone. The Twelve Steps in all their quiet nobility are what we have to keep us here today, and today, and today. And for as long as we live.

If we know that by using the lens of our dreams we can watch our addictions at work in us and also watch ourselves healing Step by Step, why would we ignore them? The answer is simple. We addicts are brilliant at rejecting and dismissing precisely what might be good for us. How often do we say something is interesting or fascinating, knowing full well that we have no intention of pursuing it? Our first impulse is to recoil from what feels like too much reality.

We consistently have to invest huge amounts of energy to keep the Steps active in our lives—meetings, connection with others in recovery, a commitment to our own inner life and our relationship to something larger than we are. We need to tell our stories again and again because we forget how lost we once were, and because these stories are the most valuable gift we have to offer to others in recovery and to the world.

Our dreams are part of our stories as well—faithful, practical, wise. They were there all along. We can choose to be put off by their mystery or we can make their story-telling a part of our own. Every time we talk about a dream we are reminded how stunningly complex we are, how wonderfully made. Whenever we actually stop to listen to a dream we also hear how deeply we yearn for health.

They will keep trying to get our attention, so how will we respond? We all know the price we have paid for staying small and impervious, swatting away all comforts and thinking we were keeping ourselves safe. It is heartbreaking that we would willfully turn away from the inner companionship that our dreams keep offering us.

The overall message of the Twelve Steps is that while we have been thrashing about trying to make sense of life, a life of meaning and purpose has been patiently trying to find us. What barriers have we put up? How can we learn to be receptive to our own inner GPS, which we loosely call intuition?

Just as the Steps point to something larger in our experience of the world, so dreams point to something larger within us. Both are invitations to grow. For each, fear can shut us down if we let it. It tells us that a wider, deeper view of ourselves doesn't really matter after all. That is precisely when we need to remind ourselves that the Steps and our dreams have our best interests at heart and that they are ultimately kind.

This book is filled with examples of dreams that illuminate, that encourage, that surprise with their insights. First, and most important, the dreamers were willing to talk about them, to take a risk and reveal parts of themselves in the hope that, by doing so, they might discover new levels of truth hiding there. Like everything else in recovery, we will be baffled by our dreams if we try to deal with them alone. What opens them up is the very fact that someone else is willing to listen to them, to devote time to them so they can expand and breathe. No special skills or training necessary— although our ability to listen can always improve with practice. Like the relationship with a sponsor, we just need a human response which involves lots of questions, real curiosity and trust that looking closely at the dream will have a practical pay-off.

What was the trigger that launched the dream? What was going on in our lives when we had it? What feelings and memories does it bring up? What are the little giveaways that defy common sense? Where are the jokes and puns? Where is the challenge? Where is the heartbeat? What striking detail gives us pause? What is the new information the dream contains? What does naming it reveal?

Not every dream has some huge revelation in it. Many are just dealing with the day-to-day, but when a dream is important we know it instinctively. It stays with us, sometimes resonates in us for months and years to come until it makes itself clear.

We do not understand consciousness. Nor do we understand the deep intuitive systems we have within us. Our addictions lied to us, promising that neither was important because we couldn't pin them down, but together they turn out to be the ground of our being, the key to having a full human experience, to living in reality.

We belong here, each one of us in our own life. As we see from those who have gone before us in Twelve Step recovery, we have the tools to face everything that life has to offer. The years add up. Change is just change and pain is just pain, but we earn the right to see it all from a new perspective.

For starters, imagine how much damage in the world has been prevented by the Twelve Steps in the many decades since they were written, and how much misery has been avoided by so many of us learning to act on our deepest levels of intuition. Imagine the relationships not destroyed, the careers not ruined, the brawls and wars not fought, the children not abused or neglected, the needless suffering and death avoided.

To get an idea of the full impact of the Twelve Steps, we just need to look at our own years in recovery to realize the amount of disaster we ourselves have avoided by staying close to our own programs, adding up the times each of us have acted in ways that reflected the best of who we are. We can then multiply our years in recovery by those of everyone in our meetings, then by the people in recovery in our society as a whole, and finally by the number of people practicing the Twelve Steps worldwide in the many decades since they have existed.

We who throughout history were dismissed as beyond hope and incurable have quietly, anonymously and almost invisibly become a powerful collective force of good for our species. Of course we have done it imperfectly, but it is fascinating to contemplate how great an impact our learning to become men and women of character has had on the whole human community. We can't point out exactly how the Twelve Steps have already changed the world, but we know from our own experience that they have.

In the same way, we can't fully explain how the small sparks of consciousness which we call dreams have within them the power to illuminate our lives, but every time we wake up and listen to them, they do.

Wayne M. is one individual in a world-wide community of people dedicated to anonymously supporting each other as we follow the Twelve Steps to recover from addictions. Personal accomplishments and our place in the world are set aside so we can feel free to speak from the heart. This commitment to anonymity allows us to speak openly about some of the most hidden and painful parts of our lives, so healing can take place within us and in those who are touched by our stories. Only with this level of honesty are we able to grow and change together.

Made in United States
North Haven, CT
08 June 2023